R 31

1st 1986

Nigel de B___

1987.

Shooting Made Easy

MIKE REYNOLDS
WITH MIKE BARNES

The Crowood Press

First published in 1986 by
THE CROWOOD PRESS
Ramsbury, Marlborough
Wiltshire SN8 2HE

British Library Cataloguing in Publication Data

Reynolds, Mike
   Shooting made easy.
   1. Trapshooting
   I. Title   II. Barnes, Mike
   799.3'13   GV1181
   ISBN 0-946284-78-4

Acknowledgements

Some photographs and diagrams are
reproduced by kind permission of *Sporting Gun.*

Front jacket photograph: Clive Nicholls
Back jacket photograph: Mike Barnes

Thanks also to Linda Bowles for her
immaculate typing.

Typeset by Alacrity Phototypesetters
Banwell Castle, Weston-super-Mare, Avon
Printed in Great Britain

Contents

Introduction

All shooting instructors have their own method of teaching. Mine is simply to teach a style of shooting which makes sense to the people who are going to use it. Most important is the need for every pupil to understand what he is doing and why he is doing it. It is pointless if you don't know exactly why you hit or missed a target. People who are waiting to take their turn on a stand at a clay shoot will often give many conflicting opinions about a shot, but it is the man or woman with the gun who should know exactly where the shot has gone in relation to the target. I therefore believe that shooting should be kept at its very simplest so that it is possible for the beginner to understand what it is all about. After all, there is nothing terribly complicated about shooting; people make it more difficult for themselves by not understanding the basics first. These basics are the reasons behind what is done and how it is done – and there is a reason for everything.

The most common fault is that of not getting in front of a bird. All shooters have enough common sense to realise that they must be in front of a bird to actually hit it, but many try to shoot a maintained lead method. As I will explain later, their approach to giving lead (or forward allowance) in this manner makes it terribly hard to achieve any sort of consistency. Also, any advice that you might hear to the effect that a given target requires 'four feet' should be completely ignored. It might appear to need four feet with a stationary gun, but as most shooters see, read and approach a target in a different way there is little point in heeding the advice.

It basically comes down to you. If you master your own approach work, the target will look after itself. The pulling of the trigger to hit the target is the simplest part. I would put my priorities in the following order: seventy per cent gun mounting, gun fit and the right chokes for the job (in that order); twenty per cent stance, weight distribution and footwork; and ten per cent reading of the target and pulling the trigger.

GUN MOUNTING AND FIT

Gun mounting and gun fit are without doubt the most important things to which you should give your attention if you wish to shoot well. Many people buy a gun and regret the decision they have made. If they had taken genuine advice from a shooting school or gunshop before buying, they would have bought a totally different weapon and, in the long term, they would have saved themselves both money and disappointment.

Don't misunderstand me, while I do have my own preference I am not saying that the actual make of gun would make the difference. What is important is to choose the right type of gun for the purpose and the job required of it. Though I don't want to get into detail at this stage, my own gun is a Browning Lightweight Game choked improved cylinder and $\frac{1}{4}$. I have had it for twelve years and it handles everything from clays (sporting and skeet) to game, pigeon and duck. This choking or perhaps $\frac{1}{4}$ and $\frac{1}{2}$ are ideal for all-round work. If you intend to specialise in trap shooting then more choke is essential. But, first of all, you must learn and master the basics. I believe all shooters should do this before they start to specialise.

You will find that most of the top competitive shots all started with either field or sporting shooting, and then chose a speciality which appealed to them.

However, to reiterate, more important than the choke are the gun mounting and fit. Unless the gun fits you properly there is little chance of making any real progress. Almost any gun can be bent to the degree needed for proper fit, so ignore any comments to the contrary. Certainly never consider any suggestion that you should adapt to a gun. It is true that some shooters do actually adapt themselves to guns, but I doubt if they shoot as well as they would if the gun fitted them properly. An experienced shot of international standard would probably be able to adapt to any gun; he would have the experience and ability to allow for the incorrect fit of a weapon. But the average person would not know that the fit was incorrect, least of all how it was affecting his shooting. The consequence of this would inevitably be inconsistent mounting and shooting. Moreover he would develop bad habits that after a few years are terribly difficult to eradicate.

The stock carries the answer to many problems. To alter the comb or cast costs little money and takes very little time, but it will make all the difference to your shooting. The point I make time and time again is that the actual shooting of a target is the part that worries people most. Whereas, in fact, if they have got everything else right it almost looks after itself! In this book I will explain how just a small measurement of half an inch out on the stock could be taking you up a blind alley, and why you may never fulfil the potential of your capability. You will also see that sustained lead plays no role in the method of shooting; and I will also consider reasons for proper gun fit, why the shape of a stock did not come about by accident and how by keeping everything simple you hold the key to success.

I will be the first to admit that we cannot all be champions. It is a fact of human nature that some will be better than others, but wouldn't you like to be just that little bit better? How many people take up the sport and make quite good progress only to reach a point where it becomes increasingly difficult to be consistent? The occasional good score gives a glimmer of hope, but the frustrations set in as a result of those all too numerous indifferent performances. You know that with consistency (particularly when related to your better days) you could be getting a great deal more satisfaction from your shooting.

There are no promises, but I'll see what I can do to help. It will all depend on how receptive you are to what I have to say. You should have no problem understanding my theories – I believe in keeping things simple. For those who have been shooting wrongly for some time, it will call for patience and hard work – but it will be worth it.

1 The Sport and its Development

Clay pigeon shooting is a super sport. It is also one which I am delighted to say has blossomed during recent years. In Norfolk, where I live, it has always had a good following, but this has not been the case throughout the country. Happily this has now changed and clubs and shooting grounds have sprung up everywhere. Sporting shooting has become the number one discipline, though as I will explain later there are nine other forms of clay sport regularly being enjoyed in the United Kingdom. It is nice to have such a variety, but I feel that this fragmentation of the sport may well be one reason why it has been slow to develop. Many other sports, such as golf, only have one form – and everyone knows it. With clay pigeon shooting there are so many varieties it is worse than explaining the rules of cricket to an American.

What is rather more easily explained, however, is the feeling you get when you pull the trigger and smash a target – the more difficult the target and the more comprehensively you break it, the greater the pleasure; and that pleasure seldom diminishes no matter how long you have been shooting. Every broken clay is a reward on its own and there are few who do not stay with the sport after breaking clays on their first attempt. Add to this the marvellous camaraderie that is part and parcel of clay pigeon shooting and it is not hard to understand why interest in the sport is increasing.

Clay pigeon shooting is all things to all people. It is a round of practice with a few friends at the local club; it is a local competition; it is about winning a place in the Great Britain team and representing your country abroad; it is about the intense personal ambition to go one better each and every time; it is about beating others and beating yourself; it is about the simple enjoyment of breaking targets. Clay pigeon shooting is whatever you want it to be, and that might be several of those things.

ORIGINS

So where did it all start? Some say America, some say England; it seems that in 1880 an American called George Ligowsky and an Englishman named McCaskey both had the same idea – to bake a target (or pigeon) of clay. There can be no doubt that both men had an incentive.

Competitive shooting at live pigeon is thought to have been in existence since the 1750s. The first club (as far as is revealed by records) was the Hornsey Wood House Pigeon Club in north London founded in 1810. Club meetings were grand social occasions, an integral part of which was the shooting. At the pull of a cord birds were released from traps situated in front of the shooter. It is interesting to note that in line with the thinking on much modern sporting and skeet shooting, the shooter could not mount his gun until the bird was in the air – even though the range was very comparable to a modern trap layout.

By the middle of the nineteenth century, with great advances being made in gun design, trap shooting was popular throughout the empire. Big money competitions took place in resorts such as Monte Carlo, and inevitably the word spread to America where, as is often the case, they did it bigger and better. The first recorded 100 straight went to an American in 1869, the legendary Captain Adam H. Bogardus who hit his 100 pigeon in a competition in St Louis Missouri.

It was at around this time, however, that live pigeon shooting started to face problems. The sheer expense and inconvenience of providing large numbers of birds, combined with the fact that anti-fieldsports lobbies of the day were starting to show opposition, meant that an alternative had to be found. The solution was glass balls. Bogardus came to the fore again and on Independence Day in 1879

A Puff Ball – an invention by Greener's made from a glass substitute which, it was claimed, emitted a cloud of 'smoke-like dust when struck'.

One of the original ball traps that threw glass balls. Special glass balls stuffed with feathers were supplied!

he broke 5,000 glass balls in 500 minutes – a staggering feat which he surpassed the following year with 6,000 from just 6,013 shots – his first miss was his 5,681st ball! It is worth noting that he used a W. & C. Scott gun. The Birmingham firm specialised in competition guns for both glass ball and live pigeon shooting, and many of the big purse European competitions were won with W. & C. Scott guns.

It goes without saying that glass was hardly the ideal material from which to make a shooting target. Apart from being expensive, awkward to handle and offering only a limited trajectory, glass balls also made a dreadful mess! In other words – the shooting world was waiting for clay pigeons. From their invention in 1880, the first tournament exclusively for clay pigeons was held in Chicago in 1884, followed in 1885 by the first national championship in New Orleans.

Meanwhile, in England, McCaskey's invention using pitch and river silt (very similar to the target still in use today) also enjoyed an automatic effect, and a new sport quickly made its presence felt. The first championship took place in Wimbledon Park in 1883.

There are six sizes of clay pigeon now available to the shoot organiser: standard, rocket, midi, mini, battue and rabbit. The rocket is not normally used in the UK but the remainder are all regularly found at sporting shoots. The standard 4¼ inch (110 mm) clay is used for skeet and trap disciplines, and

STANDARD
PATENT CLAY PIGEONS
AND TRAPS.

Ready for the Healthy Entertainment of Guests at a moment's notice.

LT.-COL. KENNEDY (Hon. Sec. of the Botley Clay Pigeon Club, Botley, Hants), says :—

"The Club was established in 1884, and have derived great amusement from the use of CLAY PIGEONS, they afford excellent sport at a very moderate price. The Club will always be willing to speak in favour of Clay Pigeons. Royal Albert Yacht Club, Southsea, February 16th, 1889."

No Country House or Military Station complete without this popular out-door Sport.

TO BE HAD OF ALL GUNMAKERS THROUGHOUT EUROPE,

AND OF THE SOLE EUROPEAN AGENTS,

LOEB & Co.,
CHURCH ALLEY,
BASINGHALL STREET, LONDON, E.C.

George Ligowsky, who is credited with being an inventor of the clay pigeon, also made traps. This particular model was recommended by Botley Clay Pigeon Club, which was apparently founded in 1884 in Botley, Hampshire.

can come in different colours. In the UK it will mainly be black or blaze depending on the background, but there are other options such as white or yellow which are used on the Continent. The midi at 90mm is a deceptive target – it looks further away than it actually is and travels faster than a standard clay. The battue is of a concave shape and has a twist and swerve in flight which can also make it awkward, often slanting edgeways on at the ideal shooting point. The mini is a trick or fun clay that is often not as difficult as it appears, while the rabbit is made differently simply because it has to travel along the ground and needs a sterner composition.

While trap shooting was the original form in which targets were shot, representing a straight translation of live pigeon trap shooting, there emerged in Britain a version which was to later be called sporting, the first championship for which was held at Perivale in 1927. Clay pigeons had, of course, given shooting schools the ideal opportunity to give clients excellent practice for their game shooting. The variety of targets thrown from the traps developed into this clay pigeon discipline called sporting.

Meanwhile, back in the States, the Davies family and a friend called Foster in Massachusetts were inventing skeet. Originally called 'shooting round the clock', the full circle of shooting positions was reduced to an arc when a neighbour became irritated by shot falling on his chicken farm. So the semi-circle was adopted. A set of rules was published in 1926, and a magazine competition for a name (which incidentally attracted some ten thousand entries) resulted in a suggestion of 'skeet' from a lady in Montana. Skeet, it transpired, was an old Scandinavian word for shoot – maybe that explains why the discipline is now so popular in Sweden and Denmark!

The clays depicted here are (top to bottom) standard, rocket, midi and mini; to the left is a battue and on the right is a rabbit.

We have come a long way – this ground in Italy has six Olympic trap layouts, with a total of eighty fully automatic underground traps. The traps are operated on an acoustic system and microphones are situated in front of each shooting station.

The battery of traps that throw clays for six layouts at the Italian ground.

DISCIPLINES

Various permutations and variations of all three forms – trap, skeet and sporting – have been developed over the passing years. I will discuss them in more detail later. While Down-the-Line, the UK's best known form of trap shooting, was originally the most popular discipline, it is sporting that now dominates clay activity in this country. This is not only understandable, but in my view perfectly correct. I have nothing against trap and skeet – in fact I enjoy both – but I am of the opinion that if anyone is to learn how to

shoot a gun he must first of all be able to prove himself competent at sporting.

With Down-the-Line or skeet you get the same targets time after time. With enough practice you can get a good score, consistently, without too much difficulty. But you may well be shooting badly and the only reason you are getting away with it is because you know where to point the gun barrels. Sporting, of course, is a different matter. Every stand will be different. A skeet target on one ground will be the same as a skeet target on another ground a hundred miles away (at least it should be), but two sporting

13

Sporting clays have become an extremely popular pastime giving enjoyment to many people. Pictured here is one of the biggest country fair shoots at Chatsworth, Derbyshire, where in the region of 1,000 entries will be taken on a six stand sporting course over a period of two days at the beginning of September.

courses only two miles apart will be completely different. To come to terms with the variety of targets with which you are likely to be presented, you will need to have mastered the basics of good shooting. Properly equipped you can then turn your hand to any discipline you wish. Not surprisingly, I will therefore concentrate our attention on sporting shooting.

2 The Gun

FIT

We should first look closely at the design of the gun and the reasons why fit is so important. We can then turn our attention to mounting in the knowledge that our adopted style of gun and shooting has not come about by accident.

I first became aware of the importance of fit when I took up competitive clay shooting. I have shot since I was a young lad, and for years had an old side-by-side that I used for rough, game and the odd session at clays. I enjoyed these occasional clay sessions, so seventeen years ago I decided to have a serious attempt at the sport and invested in what I thought was a nice over-under that would be ideal for the job. I bought a Franchi; it was a super gun, but I could not shoot as well with it as I would have liked. I presumed that I was at fault, until I was at a shoot with Wally Sykes (one of Britain's best known sporting and skeet shots) and borrowed his Browning 30 inch. Wally's gun had been altered to fit him – his alterations obviously suited me too, for I shot three times better with it than my own gun. This could not have been coincidence, so I put the two guns side by side and discovered that the drop on the stock of my gun was half an inch lower. The drop is the distance between the stock and an imaginary line level with the barrel rib. I had mine bent up by the same measurement and immediately was able to shoot every bit as well with it as I had done with Wally's. Just because a gun costs a lot of money, looks nice and is probably very well made, it does not mean that you can automatically shoot well with it.

It is common sense that we are all made and built differently, and so one specific type of gun will not suit everyone. If you bear in mind that most of the guns sold in this country are built abroad then this argument has even stronger significance. I think the manufacturers should be more interested in the needs of the people who are buying their

I found that the measurement of Wally Sykes' (above) gun suited me perfectly. Wally is one of our great shots, who in a single year won three cars outright – he is also exceptionally keen on gun fit and is never satisfied until he knows that the fit is exactly right.

15

guns – a choice in stock dimensions on different models would be a simple answer to the problem. I find that too many people adapt their style to the shape of the gun. Some shooters do this quite successfully, but even they are selling themselves short. Bad habits will develop that will inevitably make certain targets unnecessarily difficult.

TYPES OF GUN

Let's take a closer look at the gun. There are three popular choices: the over-under, side-by-side or semi-automatic. To my mind, however, there is only one choice – the over-under! The legendary John Moses Browning perfected the over-under configuration in 1926 with his Browning B25, the design of which is still very much the same today. Over the years it has been the inspiration to gunmakers throughout the world.

The over-under proved itself to be absolutely ideal for clay pigeon shooting (and in my opinion is the perfect design for all shooting). In all its shapes and forms it has the advantage of extra weight combined with what is termed as 'pointability'. The side-by-side is a super gun for driven birds, but it cannot match the over-under's versatility. Its lack of weight makes it difficult to

maintain a smooth swing and it will be inclined to be nervous or jumpy on many of the types of target seen on modern sporting layouts.

The side-by-side is an attractive gun and nice to use for driven game, but it will not fare so well on clays where its lack of weight and the barrel configuration does not meet the demands of the wide variety of targets.

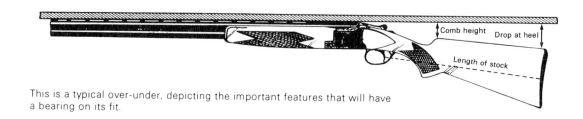

This is a typical over-under, depicting the important features that will have a bearing on its fit.

Of course, there are shots who perform magnificently with a side-by-side. One of the greatest clay shots of all time was Percy Stanbury who always shot a 30 inch Webley & Scott side-by-side. But it is worth noting that he opted for longer barrels to give him that extra steadiness on longer targets. I have little doubt that if Percy was doing all his shooting nowadays instead of fifty years ago, he would be an over-under man like the rest of the top shots. As a rough guideline I would estimate that if any of our best shots were to shoot the same hundred bird course with both an over-under and a side-by-side, their score with the former would be in the region of four to six targets higher; and that is allowing for them being a regular user of both.

When people come to my shooting school and show surprise at my use of an over-under for all shooting, I offer a simple reply: 'You don't still see farmers doing their ploughing by horse!' Times have changed and you have to take advantage of innovations that offer improvement.

I am not a great lover of semi-automatics. There are some who use them to great effect. One of our best shots of recent times is Duncan Lawton who with a Remington 1100 has won just about every title there is to be had, including a World Championship. So the guns are definitely effective. My reservations about autos, however, are on two grounds. They have a bad track record for proving faulty – nothing serious, but they have a nasty knack of jamming when you might be in the middle of ten crucial targets. Plus, of course, it is easier for an inexperienced shot to be unsafe with an auto than any other gun.

When not in use the gun bolt should always be in the open position, but even so it can be disconcerting knowing that the autos cannot be broken. This can happen more easily when a confused novice is actually in the shooting position – he might have taken his first shot, then turned round to seek advice. I have seen one or two swing the barrels of their loaded guns around with them – and it is not a pretty sight! Even worse, I have a friend who was actually shot in such an instance. He was seriously injured and very lucky not to be killed. You cannot, of course, blame the gun for such an incident – it was the person holding it who pulled the trigger. The point I am making is that the

Duncan Lawton is a superb shot and winner of a host of titles, including the World FITASC Sporting Championship. He always uses a Remington 1100 semi-automatic and proves what a winner it can be in the right hands. Yet, despite this and the fact that they are relatively inexpensive, I am not a great lover of these guns. Because they have so many moving points, they have a track record of going wrong, often at the most inopportune moment.

likelihood of this happening is increased just that little bit more when an auto is involved.

So, in conclusion, I would recommend that if anyone wants to take up clay pigeon shooting he should invest in an over-under shotgun.

Makes of gun

I would not recommend any particular make of gun other than to advise you to buy the best you can afford. I would also consider it best to buy one of the better known makes and resist the impulse to purchase what might appear to be a good bargain. With guns, like everything else in life, you get what

you pay for. There are enough good makes on the market and the most popular are Browning, Beretta, Winchester and Miroku. It is possible to get particularly good value on any of these – all are made to a comparable high standard. As guns last a lifetime you might consider a second-hand purchase, in which case it might even be possible to buy a Perazzi, if you so wish.

There are also a number of less well-known makes that have decent guns at a cheaper price – Rizzini, Lanber, Laurona, Fabarm, Franchi and Zoli are all good examples. Shop around, as you will find variations in the figure and quality of wood on stocks and, if you are buying second-

Barry Simpson favours 30 inch barrels on his Beretta, and having won the British Championship twice and the World Championship he is in a good position to advocate this length. My own feeling is that it is better for most people to come to terms with the sport by using a 27½ or 28 inch. They could switch to a longer gun at a later date.

hand, also in the general condition of the gun. Having decided on a reputable make, you will choose a sporting model (as opposed to trap, skeet or field) and the following are some of the factors to be borne in mind.

LENGTH OF BARREL

The barrel length is extremely important. The most popular is 27½ inches or 28 inches, either of which is ideal not only for sporting, but also for skeet and field shooting. Shorter barrelled guns are difficult to use. Churchill pioneered a 25 inch game gun – it is a nice looking little weapon but you need a lot of patience to become consistently good with it. I had one once and it took seven months before I got used to it. There was also a phase when 26 inch skeet guns became popular, though this is not generally the case nowadays.

A current trend is the option of 30 inch barrels. These have come into their own with the advent of sporting shoots putting on long distance targets of all sorts. In such instances the longer barrelled gun is much easier to control and will give you a steadier swing. Barry Simpson, A. J. 'Smoker' Smith and Philip Thorrold are just three of the well-

Paddy Howe has probably won more sporting titles than most and has almost exclusively used a 27½ inch gun.

known names in sporting competition circles who favour 30 inch barrels. But, in spite of this, I would suggest that all three are very accomplished performers, and for someone new to the sport a 27½ inch or 28 inch will prove a far more versatile first buy. Paddy Howe, for instance, who has won all sorts of British and European titles has never needed any more barrel length than this. Having reached a high standard, you might perhaps be in a better position to judge whether 30 inch barrels will be an advantage to you.

It will not matter whether there are one or two sights on the barrel – some have a bead site at the muzzle end and another positioned midway. The type of rib is also not very important – I personally favour a game rib rather than a very broad one. I would also recommend that you avoid buying a gun with a high post rib for sporting shooting. They are fine for trap, but I have yet to be convinced of their adaptability to other types of target.

CHOKE

I will explain later how the choke works, at this stage I will simply say that it is the amount of constriction in the end of the barrels that decides the spread of shot.

It is extremely important to have the correct chokes for your shooting. Most new guns bought off the shelf tend to be tightly choked, and although some manufacturers offer alternative choking most guns are still not suitable for the average shot. To be fair to the manufacturers this is understandable, for while the individual can have choke taken out to his preference, he cannot have it put back!

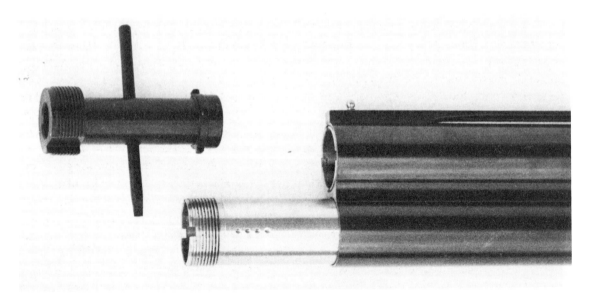

The advent of the multi-choke has been a major innovation of recent times. For sporting shooting I feel that the multi-choke in general offers the shooter little more than a conventional sporting gun with improved/¼ or ¼/½ chokings, although I can see the appeal of owning such a gun and their success is understandable. Depicted is a Beretta – the Italian firm perfected the idea of 'invisible' chokes that are simply screwed into the end of the barrel. Once in place you cannot tell that a gun offers this facility.

The multi-choke is another option, and since its introduction to the UK market by Winchester in 1980, the multi-choke seems to have taken the market by storm.

All of the major makers now produce guns with screw-in chokes, so that you can select the choke of your choice for any particular stand or discipline. The theory of this is that it is no longer necessary to own more than one gun. In many respects this is true, but personally I am not particularly in favour of switching guns anyway. The fact that you can choose a choke for different stands also raises a few doubts. While I can see the theoretical advantage, I believe that for someone trying to come to terms with the sport there is already enough to think about without deciding which choke would be most ideally suited to any given target. This can easily complicate the issue and leave the shooter not only with a muddled mind but also subconsciously expecting rather too much of his choke. Admittedly, they have some advantage to the person who maybe wants to shoot some DTL, but for trap a high shooting gun is called for as much as the choke. Perhaps mine is a voice in the wilderness and I am the last to spoil the fun of others, so all I will add is that if you like it and it suits you, then buy it!

If a gun is very tightly choked it is a bit like trying to hit a moving target with a rifle – and that isn't easy! If the target is under thirty yards away (and a large percentage will be) the pattern will not have time to have developed from a tight choke. You might get a superb 'sack of smoke' kill on a close target, but there is a greater likelihood that you will miss it altogether. Some people seem to be under the impression that their tight choke is worth keeping because it will give them good kills at extreme range. I wouldn't disagree – but why have a gun capable of killing at fifty yards when most of the targets are taken at less than thirty?

For my own gun I would opt for improved cylinder in one barrel and $\frac{1}{4}$ choke in the other. Some might like a little more at $\frac{1}{4}$ and $\frac{1}{2}$ but there is really little need for any more than that. At 25 yards for example, an improved cylinder will have a good killing pattern of more than a foot wider than a full choke. The advantage should be given to the shooter, not the target. Let's keep it easy.

FORE-END

This is very much down to individual preference. Some (including myself) prefer a nice tapered fore-end, while others opt for a clump beavertail. The important thing is that it feels right to the person holding it.

STOCK

This is a crucial part of your gun – and I am not talking about its looks, even though nicely figured walnut will always be a strong selling point.

The length of the stock will decide where your face fits, and this should be approximately an inch and a half from the comb. The actual decision on stock length will be made in conjunction with mounting (which we will discuss later). You would, of course, be well advised to have measurements taken by a qualified instructor, as I have known many people simply walk into a gun shop and proceed to mount a gun in a totally different way to which they normally shoot. The shop proprietor is not to know that the customer is deviating from his normal style and consequently cannot help but provide a gun with the wrong stock measurements.

Another misconception is that your stock length can be decided by holding the gun-

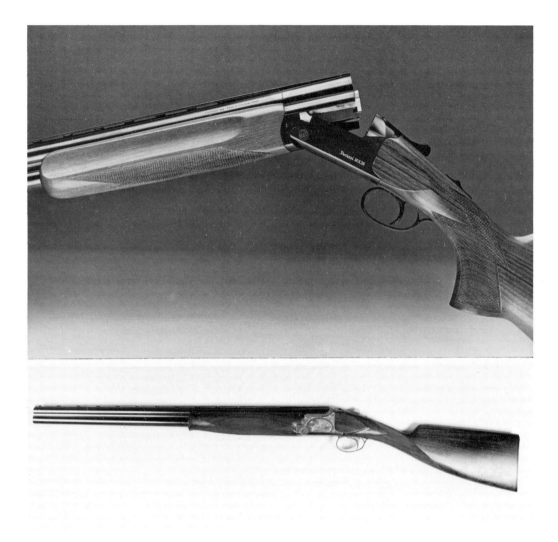

These photographs clearly show the difference between a beavertail and a tapered fore-end. (Top) A Perazzi with a beavertail fore-end; this shape is mostly found on trap and skeet guns. (Bottom) A Browning sporting model showing a tapered fore-end; in fact it has a 'tulip' curl at its tip, a popular feature on these guns. Sometimes the taper is rounded off at the end with a knurl – this is called a schnabel fore-end.

stock at the elbow and reaching for the trigger. This may work out right – it may not. What really governs the length of the stock is the size of the neck and depth of the cheekbone. The stock length is the distance between the middle of the butt of the stock and the point at which the finger pulls the trigger. The angle at the end of the stock is known as 'stand' and is shaped to fit the shoulder – though apart from some being a little pointed at the toe (bottom end), this does not generally prove a problem area.

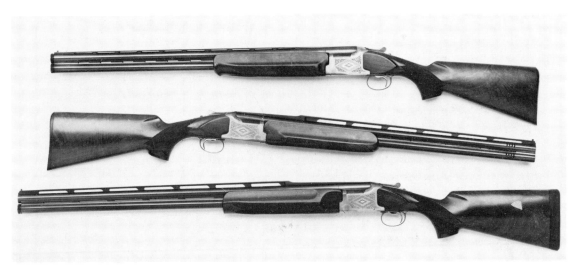

These three Winchester Diamond Grade guns show the variety in styles. The top gun is a sporting model with a tapered fore-end (the knurl at its end often lends it the name of tulip or schnabel fore-end). The middle gun is a skeet gun and has a thick beavertail fore-end. The bottom model is a trap gun and has a slight taper – in fact the majority of trap models feature beavertail.

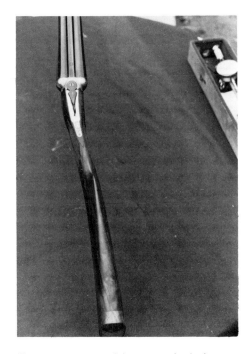

The cross-over stock is one method of overcoming the problem of a left master eye for a right-handed person. I personally feel that it would be easier and better to learn to shoot off the left shoulder.

COMB

The height of the gun is possibly the most important measurement. A shotgun differs from a rifle where you have both a fore sight and a rear sight. If you line the two up on the target there is a very strong chance you will hit it. With a shotgun your cheekbone acts as the rear sight. In either sporting or skeet shooting the comb of the shotgun should be adjusted so that when the cheekbone is sitting on the stock, you should be looking straight down the barrel, and the rib should be visible, but only just.

Most guns should shoot one-third on and below the target and two-thirds above. This means that the gun will shoot slightly above your aim and that you need never lose sight of the target. This is the method of shooting that I teach and it seems to work pretty well. Some prefer to blot a target, but the point I make is that it is very difficult to consistently hit a target that you cannot see. With a gun fitted on the above basis, the only target which is unsighted is the overhead driven, and as the gun is shooting a little high you have already got a built-in advantage on that one.

The magic figure for the distance between the comb and the parallel with the barrels is once again an inch and a half. The drop at the heel (the top of the end of the stock) will be around two inches, or perhaps two and a quarter inches. I shoot an inch and a half and two inches as do several other people I know.

While you will find that most new guns have a comb height of around an inch and a half, their drop at heel can vary between two and a quarter to three inches. I have had to push a stock as far as three-quarters of an inch to get it right.

CAST

Many shooters are under the illusion that the cast on a stock (the degree to which the stock

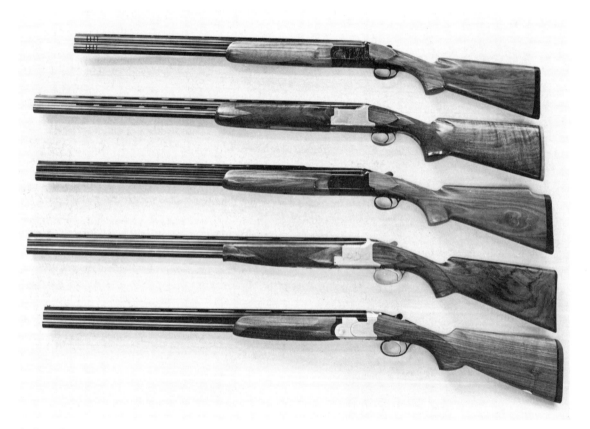

At first glance one over-under may appear very similar to the next, but take a close look at this photograph. The five guns depicted are (top to bottom) a Perazzi Skeet with 27 inch barrels and cooling slots (an occasional feature on top competition models); a Winchester Grand European Montecatini Trap 30 inch; a Perazzi 30 inch Trap with two features that can often be found in trap models – a stepped rib and a Monte Carlo stock (note the step in front of the heel of the stock); a Browning A3 Special Sporting 30 inch with a slim tulip fore-end; and a Beretta 28 inch Sporting.

moves away from the line of the barrels) will eradicate all eye problems. Unfortunately this is not true. Cast is generally built into or added to a stock to enable the shooter to mount the gun correctly. Shooters with short necks and stocky build will benefit the most from a degree of cast in their guns.

If a person has a dominant left eye his options are:

1. To shoot with a full cross-over stock.

2. To shoot from the left shoulder.
3. To close his left eye, which will automatically solve the problem.
4. To use a centre vision stock, which has an inch and a half cast that will put the line of the gun between the two eyes.

To return to the third point, you will quite rightly hear that it is best to shoot with both eyes open, but this is not possible if you are not capable of doing so. Some say that you

Now look at the differences in comb height of the same five guns. Note that the two sporting models (Browning left and Beretta centre) have the most drop, which means that they will shoot to the point of aim. The Browning here looks as though its comb height is a little too high and you would have to obscure the target in order to hit it. The Perazzi Skeet gun (second left) looks about right. Both the two trap guns (far right) have minimal drop, which means that they will shoot high, and you would need to see all of the target in order to hit it (which is the case for many shooters in the specialist fast trap disciplines). The photograph demonstrates that it is almost impossible to buy a gun off the shelf and expect it to fit you as they vary so much. Alteration, however, is a simple job.

don't get a proper field of vision with one eye closed, but as it is generally not necessary to close the eye until shortly before pulling the trigger, I cannot see the strength of such an argument. If you have an excessive degree of pull from the left eye, close it and your kills ratio will improve. It is as simple as that.

In conclusion there will be anything from half to three-quarters of an inch cast on a gun, depending on the build of the individual.

TRIGGERS

Choose a gun with a single selective trigger (i.e. just one trigger and the option to fire whichever barrel you wish) – there is usually a barrel selector on the safety catch. Double triggers can be a bit of a nuisance for clay pigeon shooting where you may need to take two shots very quickly.

It is also worth checking the trigger pulls – this is the amount of resistance the trigger offers before it will release the striker. It is measured in pounds. For sporting shooting these should ideally be set up at $3\frac{1}{2}$ lb on the front trigger and $4\frac{1}{4}$ lb on the back – 'front' and 'back' in the instance of single triggers refer to the mechanism not the actual trigger itself. Top Olympic trap competitors prefer a much lighter trigger pull so that they can respond almost instinctively to seeing the target. In sporting, however, if the pulls are too light they can cause the shooter to squeeze before he is really ready – and if they are too heavy he will hang on to his shot and pull the barrels down from the target.

Trigger pulls can vary enormously. I had someone at the ground recently whose brand new gun had 9 lb trigger pulls. This tends to be more of a problem on cheaper guns where the weight of the pull will be dependent on both the quality of the workman who made it

and the materials available. A cheaper gun will probably have poorer quality metal with more give.

WEIGHT

You often hear people say that they like a nice light gun, but it should be remembered that a Purdey will weigh in at around $6\frac{3}{4}$ lb to 7 lb. So even the most aristocratic of gunmakers don't go in for the featherweight class.

While no one wants to use a gun that is too heavy to hold, it should have enough weight to absorb recoil. If the gun does not take the recoil the shooter will – and apart from the fact that undue recoil is not particularly pleasant, it is also off-putting when it comes to taking a second shot. I would suggest that a weight of around 7 lb to $7\frac{1}{4}$ lb will provide the right kind of compromise. People who find it difficult to cure a flashing of the gun (i.e. they cannot maintain a nice smooth swing), may benefit from a little more weight. Beretta are now making sporting guns of around 8 lb.

The weight element, incidentally, is one of the advantages that the over-under has over the side-by-side. If you use anything over an ounce load in a side-by-side you get too much recoil and you will find that muzzle flip will ruin second-barrel shots. The over-under is a steadier and easier gun to use.

CLEANING

It goes without saying that when you buy your gun you should also invest in a cleaning kit. With just a little regular attention, your gun will give you a lifetime's service and, unlike most other things which you buy, it will hold its price.

3 Cartridges and Choke

CARTRIDGES

It is important to have good cartridges, and there are a number of well-known firms producing top quality cartridges at comparable prices. Some people might argue that they can find a cheaper brand, but really price just doesn't come into it. If you buy in bulk of a thousand or more (maybe with a group of friends), the cost for each shooting trip is only marginally more than if you used the cheapest brand available. You will find this especially applicable if you decide to take part in big competitions, where far more money will be spent on entry fees, travel, food and possibly accommodation. Remember you only get what you pay for – and sometimes you don't get that! My advice is to always go for a well-known reliable brand that will give consistent shooting. Make your choice and stick to it. After a period of time you will get used to a particular cartridge and intuitively know its capabilities. Therefore you can ignore any talk you might hear from people at a competition suggesting that a particular bird might need a heavy load or some special fast bomber! These people are rather expecting their cartridges to do their shooting for them. It never quite works like that!

Sizes

Normally in sporting shooting you will have with you your chosen brand in sevens and nines, thus giving you the option for close or long range targets. I have tended to use a lot of skeet (nine) cartridges, but now several of the top clay competitors favour eights for all targets, other than those which are extremely close. This has come about with the advent of the availability of eight loads by all the major manufacturers. It is a nice size and lends further weight to the theory that you can get used to one load to the extent that you fully know its capabilities.

It is interesting that many people assume that the top quality trap loads give those special 'cloud of dust' kills because they are incredibly fast. Yet the real reason for this is that they use harder shot which is less prone to distortion and consequently gives a tighter pattern. Conversely, soft shot will give a nice open pattern, which can in fact be beneficial for general sporting shooting.

What you should do is take your chosen brand and gun to a pattern plate. Try the different shot sizes from twenty, thirty and forty yards so that you get a fair idea of what you can expect from your gun and cartridge combination. Having done this, you can then enter a competition in the knowledge that you are properly equipped to deal with any of the targets presented to you. Once you have made a decision about gun and cartridges, stick with the combination for quite a while before you entertain the idea of changing. Even the most experienced shots can take anything up to five thousand shells to get used to a new gun or change of cartridge.

Velocity and Pattern

While on paper their velocities may show only a marginal variance (we are probably talking about a difference of 1,100 and 1,110 feet per second between different makes) the characteristics of the different loads might be

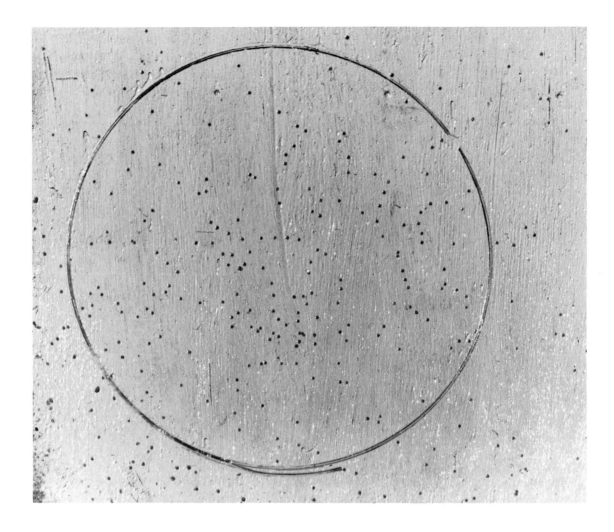

quite distinct. Some are heavy on recoil, others have tight patterns, the noise might be different – all these factors combine for a factual and psychological effect on the man pulling the trigger.

The fastest trap cartridges on the market are SMI Master Trap or Olympionica and Fiocchi VIP 3 – all at around 1,155 feet per second. These will feel pretty powerful in a standard sporting gun. They are fast with tight patterns and designed specifically for trap shooting. Look instead to one of the many regular brands on the market such as Eley Olympic, Winchester Trap 100,

Maionchi (which I use), Dan Arms, Fiocchi VIP 1, Victory, Rottweil CX – they are all well recommended. Choose a 1⅛oz load.

Shot with nickel plating inhibits cold welding of pellets and thus helps to produce superior patterns, chiefly of value to top level clay competitors. This is expensive shot and not generally necessary.

It may seem an unusual yardstick, and it is probably coincidental, but it seems that the more you pay the tighter the pattern. So check the pattern plate to see how the chokes are functioning with your chosen brand.

Left and below The kinds of patterns that are produced. The circles are 30 inches in diameter and have been drawn on a pattern plate set at 40 yards in order to test two trap loads with a full choke gun. The photograph on the left features a home load of rather soft shot, while the other pattern is from a specialist trap load. The home load shows a 52 per cent pattern, while the factory competition load produced 70 per cent – the difference in density is purely because of the hardness of the shot. Generally, better quality cartridges feature harder shot which gives more consistent patterns. Competition trap loads can give those tight patterns that will 'smoke' a clay and also carry plenty of pattern power at extreme range.

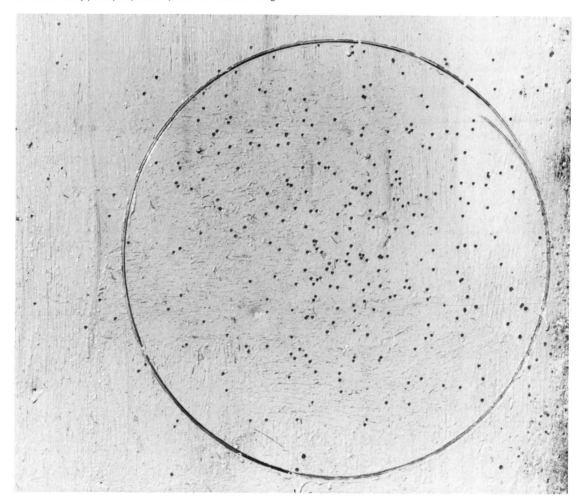

CHOKES

To get a fair idea of how a choke works, imagine a garden hose – if you squeeze it at the end the water stays forceful and concentrated, and you can aim at a distance. If on the other hand you leave it wide open then the water comes out in a nice thick gush, but has no far-reaching penetration. Similarly a tight choke of ¾ or full will give tight patterns at a distance and an open choke will offer a nice open spread closer to the gun.

CONSTRICTION APPLIES RADIAL PRESSURE

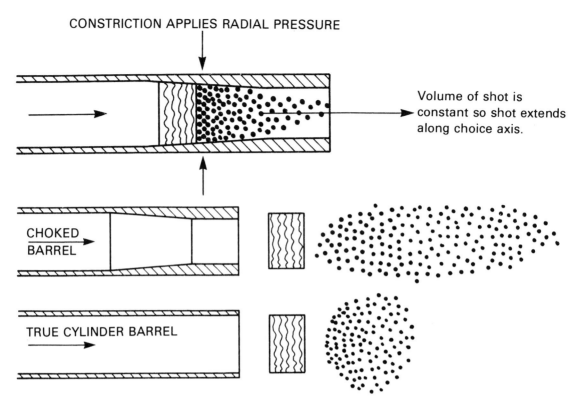

Volume of shot is constant so shot extends along choice axis.

CHOKED BARREL

TRUE CYLINDER BARREL

Comparison of shot string from choked and true cylinder barrels (exaggerated view).

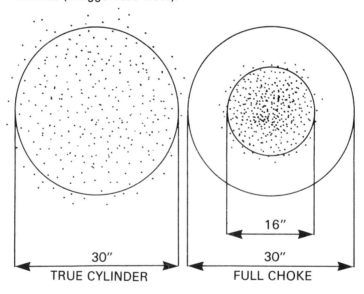

16"

30"

TRUE CYLINDER

30"

FULL CHOKE

How it works – the shot leaving the muzzle of the barrel.

As I mentioned earlier, I personally favour a gun with open chokings for sporting shooting as the majority of the targets will be well within the capability of such a gun. This is particularly so with modern plastic wad cartridges which throw a very much tighter pattern than fibre or felt wad loads. Also, as we have decided to use a good quality make, these will inevitably also carry shot of a good hardness and consequently further encourage a tighter pattern. In other words, the shot pattern is likely to be plenty tight enough without the encumbrance of a tight choke.

The accompanying tables taken from the Eley Shooter's Diary further highlight the differences in cartridge behaviour and show the kind of ballistics that one can expect. Incidentally, I would recommend that anyone taking up the sport has this diary each year. It is an excellent little publication and contains much useful information.

Choke is effectively a funnel or forcing cone found at the muzzle end of the barrel which reduces the diameter of the bore by up to 45 thousandths of an inch over anything up to the last six inches of the barrel (in the case of a 12-bore). The more usual choke length however is one and a half to two and a half inches. The amount of constriction in the choke will determine the pattern density which we can expect that barrel to produce. For example, a full choke barrel should place seventy per cent plus of its shot charge into a thirty inch circle at forty yards – a true cylinder (no choke) should place about forty per cent into the same circle at the same distance.

Shot String

Numerous experiments have been carried out in an attempt to measure both pattern and string. An American once even put a

Shot Sizes (nominal)				
Desig-nation	Diameter		Pellets	
	mm	in	per 10 g	per oz
LG	9.1	.36	2	6
SG	8.4	.33	3	8
Spec. SG	7.6	.30	4	11
SSG	6.8	.27	5½	15
AAA	5.2	.20	12½	35
BB	4.1	.16	25	70
1	3.6	.14	36	100
3	3.3	.13	50	140
4	3.1	.12	60	170
5	2.8	.11	78	220
6	2.6	.10	95	270
7	2.4	.095	120	340
7½	2.3	.09	140	400
8	2.2	.085	160	450
9	2.0	.08	210	580

Number of Pellets in Shot Load (nominal)							
Weight of shot		Size of shot					
g	oz	3	4	5	6	7	8
46	1⅝	228	276	358	439	552	732
42.5	1½	210	255	330	405	510	675
36	1¼	175	213	275	338	425	562
34	1³⁄₁₆	166	202	261	321	404	534
32	1⅛	157	191	248	304	383	506
30	1¹⁄₁₆	149	181	234	287	361	478
28.5	1	140	170	220	270	340	450
26.5	¹⁵⁄₁₆	131	159	206	253	319	422
25	⅞	122	149	193	236	298	394
23	¹³⁄₁₆	113	138	179	219	276	366
17.5	⅝	87	106	138	169	212	282
16	⁹⁄₁₆	78	96	124	152	191	254
12.5	⁷⁄₁₆	61	75	97	118	149	187
9	⁵⁄₁₆	44	53	69	84	106	141

The tables above and overleaf highlight the differences in cartridge behaviour. Clay shooters should note that they are allowed to use shot sizes six to nine for their sport. In fact, there is no advantage from using anything else, and I would never use a six for clays.

huge pattern plate on the side of a train! The capability of a cartridge is a fascinating subject which will always cause debate, but for the time being I would suggest that you don't get bogged down in too much detail. I mention the basic facts here so that you can have an understanding of what it is all about.

In layman's terms an open choked barrel will throw a broad pattern of only a smallish depth (relatively little shot string), while a tight choke will keep the pattern tight and consequently there will be a very much longer shot string (remember the hose pipe with the squeezed end).

In theory, therefore, if you shoot well in front of a target with a tight choke you will be increasing your chances of hitting the clay as it will have a very much longer shot string with which to collide. That may be the case in theory, but when you consider that the shot is travelling faster than the speed of sound the margin of error becomes a much more significant factor. My advice, therefore, is to forget about shot string and simply stick to a gun, choke and cartridge combination that will throw a nice open and evenly distributed pattern.

Percentage of total pellets in 30 inch circle									
Boring of gun	Range in yards								
	20	25	30	35	40	45	50	55	60
True Cylinder	80	69	60	49	40	33	27	22	18
Improved Cylinder	92	82	72	60	50	41	33	27	22
¼-Choke	100	87	77	65	55	46	38	30	25
½-Choke	100	94	83	71	60	50	41	33	27
¾-Choke	100	100	91	77	65	55	46	37	30
Full Choke	100	100	100	84	70	59	49	40	32

It is possible to calculate the number of pellets in a 30 inch circle for any shot size and in any of the six borings of gun at the ranges stated simply by using the tables on page 31.

Diameter of spread							
Boring of gun	Range in yards						
	10	15	20	25	30	35	40
True Cylinder	20	26	32	38	44	51	58
Improved Cylinder	15	20	26	32	38	44	51
¼-Choke	13	18	23	29	35	41	48
½-Choke	12	16	21	26	32	38	45
¾-Choke	10	14	18	23	29	35	42
Full Choke	9	12	16	21	27	33	40

The figures show the diameter of spread in inches covered by the bulk of the shot.

Forward Allowance

Birds crossing at 65 kmph (40 mph)										
Range	30m	30yd	35m	35yd	40m	40yd	45m	45yd	50m	50yd
Standard Velocity	1.89m	5ft 6in	2.26m	6ft 8in	2.68m	8ft	3.29m	9ft 6in	3.97m	11ft 1in
High Velocity	1.81m	5ft 3in	2.18m	6ft 5in	2.58m	7ft 8in	3.16m	9ft 1in	3.02m	10ft 8in

Forward allowance. Eley standard game loads have a nominal velocity of 325 metres per second (1,070 feet). Eley high velocity loads have a nominal velocity of 340 metres per second (1,120 feet). One might suppose that the change in velocity would make a noticeable difference to the forward allowance, but, as will be seen from the table, the question is one of inches in a forward allowance measured in feet. The difference may, for all practical purposes, be ignored.

4   The Disciplines

There are three principal forms of clay pigeon shooting favoured in this country today – English sporting, English skeet and Down-the-Line. All are unique to the United Kingdom.

ENGLISH SPORTING

This has become by far the most popular form of clay pigeon shooting with a 100 bird British Open Championship that attracts around 1,000 entries each May – and there are 1,800 entries for the thirty target Game Fair Championship at the end of July. Its appeal is obvious. Variety really is the spice of life when it comes to English sporting and that's the way it should be, for the principal idea of the discipline is to simulate the flight of quarry birds in the field. It is also less expensive for a club to stage as no permanent buildings or trap houses are required. A club will instead make use of the natural contours or cover provided by their shooting area to

A 'driven pheasant' stand at an English sporting competition – sporting is by far the most popular discipline.

supply such targets as crossing pigeon, driven pheasant and springing teal. These stands are straightforward translations of the real thing. Even if a club has only a bare flat field, with a little imagination it can still create an enjoyable little shoot. The use of straw bales to protect the trappers and scaffolding from which to throw higher birds are popular aids that are used to great effect. Of course, it is nicer to have completely natural surroundings but this is not always possible.

Stands

Virtually all clubs, no matter how big or small, will put on a shoot to include several stands – even a twenty-five bird event usually has three stands – offering a variety of targets to the shooter. He also gets very spoilt in that, unlike his game or field counterpart, during a year he will have had countless opportunities at rights and lefts!

Most stands consist of ten birds – hence three stands for a thirty bird competition. Although if a club has the available equipment and manpower this might rise to four, with three stands of eight targets and the other with six. The nature of these stands is always an unknown quantity, but, for example, they could be as follows:

Stand One – four pairs of driven.
Stand Two – fur and feather; perhaps a bolting rabbit followed by a low quartering hedge hopper.
Stand Three – springing teal, on report (a single target is followed by another similar single released on the sound of gunfire at the first).
Stand Four – crossing pigeon, on report (a crossing target at maybe twenty-five yards).

High tower birds are always very popular.

Clearly, with so many different types of clay, both in trajectory and also size (standard, midi, mini, battue and rabbit), the shooter will always be presented with an enjoyable challenge.

Learning ground

Sporting, because of its variety, offers the perfect learning ground for anyone with aspirations of becoming a good shot. He may later like to try his hand at game shooting and will find that his clay sport has been the perfect preparation. Indeed, he will discover it to be a much easier proposition than his game shooting counterpart switching to clays. A good clay shot will almost always shoot well at game, but a good game shot often finds clays awkward at first. This is mainly as a result of the factors that I am trying to highlight – wrong gun, bad gun fit and substandard mounting.

Don't get me wrong, I'm not saying that the game shooters don't know how to shoot. I know some excellent shots who never tackle clays. The point I am making is that there is much more variety in clay shooting than, for instance, on a driven pheasant shoot, and a fast flying clay target will quickly highlight problems that may never have previously shown themselves in the shooting field, particularly for someone who has just four or five outings a year.

ENGLISH SKEET

This discipline consists of two targets on fixed flightlines released from two trap houses and shot from seven different stations positioned in a semi-circle. During a round you will encounter a whole variety of targets – on Station One, for instance, you get a going away bird coupled with a low driven.

Consequently, many use skeet as a training ground for all their later shooting. While in principle this is fine and certainly you can learn gun handling and familiarity, once you have passed this stage you tend to learn less about shooting and more about breaking skeet targets. You know where each and every target is coming from and where it is travelling to – so you could still get a good score with a suspect style. Having said that, it is nevertheless a very enjoyable form of shooting.

DOWN-THE-LINE

This is the classic 'beginner' discipline for going away targets. I am sure that its supremos won't mind me calling it that, for the modest speed, minimal target variance of DTL birds and gun-up shooting position combine to present the novice with the opportunity of returning a decent score. However, while DTL gives the novice a chance of quickly achieving scores in excess of seventy-five per cent, becoming a winner in the discipline is a different matter and requires tremendous dedication and great powers of concentration.

English skeet has a good following; its seven different shooting stations offer a variety of targets and are a great aid to consistent mounting.

Down-the-Line is all about concentration, a vital ingredient to all consistent shooting.

OTHER DISCIPLINES

There are seven other disciplines which are all actively enjoyed by British shooters.

FITASC Sporting

Although it is expensive to stage, this discipline has a terrific appeal. It is discussed in detail in Chapter 9.

ISU skeet

This is a faster form than our own English version, and is shot throughout Europe and at the Olympic Games. Competitors start with gun down, and there is a delay on release of the target of up to three seconds. The discipline features an eighth station, situated between the two trap houses.

Olympic trap

This is the other Olympic clay discipline; North Country vet Bob Braithwaite won a gold medal in the Mexico Olympics of 1968. This is the hardest of the trap disciplines with three traps in front of each shooting position, throwing clays of widely differing angles to seventy-five metres plus at varying speeds that can exceed ninety miles per hour. It has its biggest following in Italy.

Universal trap or trench

This has similar targets and speeds to Olympic trap but there are only five traps involved. It is another very challenging discipline, and is popular in France, Holland and Spain.

Automatic Ball Trap (ABT)

Some claim this to be a midway house from DTL to Olympic trap – I suspect that it is nearer to the latter than the former. Again it is a challenging form of trap shooting. There is just one trap, auto-angling providing a wide range of targets at fairly fast speeds.

One of our top ISU skeet shots, Paul Bentley, in action at the Los Angeles Olympics.

Olympic trap – the photograph was taken on one of the many superb grounds to be found on the continent. Like ISU skeet, as its name suggests, this is an Olympic discipline.

Pro-trap

This is not really a trap discipline, but quite a new sport involving the use of seven traps releasing clays in a computerised sequence so that a shooter from one position will rattle off at twenty-five clays from all kinds of angles. It is very exciting to shoot, but can be inconvenient to stage.

Starshot

This is the very latest clay game to hit the scene. It was devised by Scottish shooter David Maxwell specifically to present television with a form of the sport that lends itself well to the small screen. It was launched in January 1986 with a Pro–Celebrity programme on BBC featuring Jackie Stewart

One of Norfolk's top shots, Steve Cooper, in action on a Pro-trap layout; the seven traps are sited at points around the layout.

The latest form of clay shooting, Starshot, takes place under floodlights.

and John Watson with top clay shots Gerry Cowler and Barry Simpson. It is shot under floodlights (to give a dramatic effect) with clays rising up a semi-circular frame positioned at ninety degrees. The clay can be in one of several upward directions and the challenge for the shooter is to break it before it reaches certain marker points.

I was fortunate to be consulted about the idea in the early planning stages and was very impressed. Although perhaps not a form of clay shooting that will attract big numbers in terms of competition, it could through television attract a lot of new people to the sport. The sport has needed something like this for a long time, and I hope that it will prove to be a success.

5 Style

BASICS

I have touched briefly on the different disciplines involved in the shooting of clay pigeons, but before exploring them further we must first master the basics.

First of all, anyone taking up shooting must understand his gun, how it is built to a specific design and why shooting in a certain manner will bring about a kill. This is absolutely fundamental.

I should now perhaps give some background to the style of shooting which I favour. It is a method which seems to work pretty well with pupils and it makes a lot of sense when it is explained. There are basically three styles of shooting:

1. The style I favour is that of tracking a bird behind and swinging through it to pull the trigger on the swing through.
2. You will also see people shoot the Churchill method, where they raise the gun, swing and shoot all in one movement.
3. There is also the sustained lead method, which involves blotting a bird out, moving in front to a given point and pulling the trigger.

You will hear strong arguments for all three, but the method I use suits me and also suits most of my pupils so that is the one I stick to. But I think that the strongest point in its favour is that it makes sense.

Tracking method

The gun fit is such that a little (and it is a very little) of the rib is visible to the eye when the gun is in position. This means that two-thirds of the pattern will be thrown above the point of aim and one-third on the target and below. Consequently it is possible to maintain a complete picture of the target during the entire process. The only exceptions to this are driven and springing teal type targets – and even on these the 'two-thirds above' gives a slight edge.

I do not claim any originality for this style of shooting. Thousands have used it over the years, including the legendary Percy Stanbury. It is not hard to see why it is such a popular style. Basically as long as the gun fit, mounting and approach work are right the shooting of the target looks after itself. It does not matter what direction the target is taking. If you pick up the line, tracking behind will give you the speed and your brain will have programmed the pulling of the trigger on the swing through. There is a minimum of mental calculation – experience and a smooth swing will give you consistency.

Mounting

Good mounting counts for so much in shooting that you cannot practise it enough. Give yourself a few minutes each day in the comfort of your own home. You don't have to shoot live cartridges to get into the habit of a nice even swing and smooth mount – simply look for an imaginary target across the room, perhaps along the line where the wall meets the ceiling. You can also look in the mirror to check that the stock is fitting correctly into your face – your eye will appear to be sitting perfectly on the rib. Incidentally, if you have the light on, make sure that you draw the curtains – your neighbour might decide to call the police!

THE METHOD

A comfortable upright stance with the eyes looking over the barrel for the target; ready to call the bird.

The bird is released and the weight goes onto the front foot as the eye picks out the target.

Top right   Still keeping the eye on the target, the gun mounting has begun. The barrels will continue to swing smoothly with the bird.

Bottom right   The gun comes up to the cheek and the eye is still firmly locked onto the target.

The gun is now in the cheek and the bird will be tracked leaving a little air showing between the muzzles and the rear of the clay. You can then swing through for a kill.

MOUNTING IN CLOSE-UP

You have just called the clay and are looking for it to appear.

The eye is seeking the target and the arms are responding with the mount.

The gun comes nearer the shoulder and the concentration remains unbroken.

The eye looks out directly over the end of the barrel towards the target as the gun reaches the shoulder.

The gun is in place. Neither the head nor the level of the end of the barrels has moved throughout the entire process. A good gun fit is therefore of paramount importance.

Stance

Your stance should be relaxed but positive with the weight taken on your front foot – left foot in the case of a right-hander and vice versa. Think how a tennis player serves off his front foot. This gives him the perfect poise and ability to pivot the top half of his body without having any detrimental effect on what he is doing. Similarly, your front foot will always be pointing in the direction in which you will hit the clay.

Do a dress rehearsal with an empty gun on an imaginary clay. It may be a right to left crosser. Face the point at which you hope to hit the clay, then keeping your feet in the

Right The correct stance – the body takes the form of a flowing arc with the weight and the balance on the left foot. It is a stylish and easy way to shoot a target.

same position move the barrels and the top half of your body to a point where the clay will appear and where you can pick it up. You will then be able to mount the gun, track, move through and kill it with complete ease at the predetermined point. Easy, isn't it!

Shooting is all about getting into good habits. You can practise this procedure time and time again until eventually you do everything without thinking. Providing your gun fit is good and you practise correctly, you will begin to mount the gun as naturally as picking up a pint!

GETTING IT RIGHT

The left leg is bent and again weight distribution is all over the place.

The following five photographs all show an incorrect stance. This is probably one of the most common of the incorrect stances.

Right It is possible to shoot off the back foot but it presents problems and movement is somewhat inhibited.

47

Too far forward – there will be a total lack of manoeuvrability.

Another back foot stance – balance is difficult to maintain.

CORRECT METHOD

One point which I cannot over-emphasise about shooting is that if your method is not correct then it will eventually catch you out. After you have been shooting a while you will know that you will be able to hit certain targets, and that number will increase with experience and practice – but only so far. If you are not doing everything correctly you will come unstuck on a good stand.

The problem can be highlighted with gifted shots, those who naturally have a very good eye and sharp senses. They will tend to shoot by instinct, perhaps neglecting a correct method and approach. If they are regularly achieving a fair success rate this is understandable, but they will inevitably lose out at some point, perhaps when they least want to. This is especially true with quick reaction shots who will intercept a target or point the gun in the general direction of its flight. It usually works, but the problem arises when it doesn't – they don't know why their ability has suddenly become fallible. Bad luck might be blamed, but it won't be the cause.

The same applies to shooters of all levels. If you find that your own scores can vary enormously, it is not simply because you are not getting enough regular practice (though this always helps) the most likely cause is that you are not going through the proper procedure of reading and shooting a target.

Assessment

Take your time and think about your shooting. Before you shoot, have a good look at a target to assess its line and speed. The same applies to game and rough shooting. Check your impulse to shoot and give yourself a couple of moments' thought to read the bird. Then mount the gun keeping your eyes on

Wrong! A common problem with back foot shooting is that the gun will drift from the face, particularly with left to right birds (or for a left-hander, right to left birds).

Right! If you have the weight on the front foot the stock will automatically sit into the face. This photograph illustrates another point – while my right eye is my master eye it is not as dominant as it should be. I therefore close my left eye at the point of taking the shot.

the bird, track it, swing through and squeeze the trigger. Avoid flashing the gun at all times.

Many guns go wrong on quartering birds, those targets that start at your side and angle inwards but away from you. Make sure that you don't take your gun back too far. If you read the bird, you will see that it travels very quickly at the start but loses pace after twenty yards. Follow it from the trap with your eyes, intercept with your mount, then track and kill it. Be deliberate and apply maximum concentration on the target, but

give yourself time. Even the fastest of targets gives you more time than you'll ever realise ... until you take it. One of the finest skeet shooters I know has the easiest of styles yet takes the targets before almost anyone else.

Correcting old habits

The main problem is that old habits die very hard. I once had a well-known sporting shot at my ground who was having difficulty with right to left crossers. We had a go on a few clays and his problem was quickly

THE CROSSER

IMPORTANCE OF FIT

(a)　　　　　　　　(b)　　　　　　　　(c)

These three illustrations give an idea of what to expect when a sporting gun is properly mounted.

(a) Wrong – nothing of the rib can be seen at all, only the top of the bead sight. This means that in many cases you will have to completely blot out the clay in order to break it.

(b) Wrong – too much of the rib is showing on this one, the consequence of which is that your shot pattern will rise above the target. This might be all right if you are shooting a quickly rising trap target, but for virtually all other shooting it would prove a handicap.

(c) Correct – just enough of the rib is showing, which means that your shot pattern will strike two-thirds on and above the target, and one third below. You will therefore be able to keep the target in view at all times.

Top left Ready to call the bird with my weight on the front foot and eyes to where the target will appear.

Top right As the target moves across my field of vision I start to use my feet to get into a good shooting position.

Bottom left Having followed the target and positioned myself, the mount is now in motion. Good footwork is important.

Bottom right Having mounted, tracked and swung through the target I pull the trigger with confidence of a kill, and still keep the barrel moving!

apparent. His style was aggressive, quick and generally it was easy to see why he had done well – but it was also clear why certain types of target caused him great problems. He really wasn't reading the birds properly, but simply shooting intuitively. It took a while for me to convince him of that – if you have done a lot of shooting quite successfully it is hard trying to shake off your style for a different one. The one target that will highlight approach work is a long driven bird, and so it proved – he broke the clays but it was a

51

LOOKING DOWN THE GUN BARREL –
keeping it smooth for a powdered clay

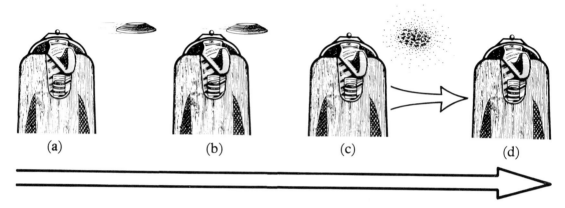

(a)   (b)   (c)   (d)

(a) The gun has been mounted and the swing brings it towards the clay.

(b) The gun is moved into a position behind the clay, the barrel level with its underside. Track the clay to find its speed and angle.

(c) Having reached the point at which it will be easiest shot, you can now swing through, the tracking having dictated the swing.

(d) Pull the trigger and keep swinging – the clay will disintegrate!

long wait followed by rush and aggression. I'll admit it took most of the afternoon and I gave him a lot of stick, but the penny eventually dropped. He relaxed, read the targets, adapted and shot some beautiful birds from a wide variety of angles, including a whole manner of right to left crossers. It was a treat to watch. So give it a little thought – take your time, apply yourself and keep it simple.

6 Clothing

COAT AND FOOTWEAR

Before you do any kind of shooting you will want to make sure you are properly dressed for the job. The shooting image of Barbour and wellies is absolutely correct for those miserable cold wet days (that we sometimes seem to get right through the year). If it is wet underfoot you will want to keep the wellies on at all times. But, to do yourself justice at clays for goodness' sake don't entertain the idea of shooting while wearing a Barbour or indeed any sort of coat.

There is little point in having a gun specially fitted only to be bundled up with clothes. 'But what about game shooters?' I hear you say, and quite rightly. The difference is that not only can it get very cold when you are out game or pigeon shooting, but when you actually see a bird there is normally enough time to achieve the desired fit in the shoulder before you take your shot. In a clay contest, however, the moment you see a target, it is travelling at its fastest and will be slipping away from you in no time. You will want to mount the gun quickly and straight into the correct spot each and every time. A bad mount spells a lost target – it is as simple as that.

A closely fitting skeet vest is the answer. I normally wear a sweater underneath to act as a little padding. Wear your Barbour by all means, but for that short period when it is your turn to shoot, remove it and rely on gun fit with your skeet vest. There is an ample choice of vests on the market. A vest with lots of pockets is always nice, though strictly there is never any need to take more than fifteen cartridges onto a stand. While the fit of the vest needs to be close, you must be sure that it isn't too tight or it could hamper your swing.

If the ground is at all firm, I would also dispense with the wellingtons and opt for some comfortable trainers. Shooting is all about comfort and ease of stance. It might be a long day in a big competition, maybe with some waiting in queues, so you won't want anything in which you are going to feel uncomfortable.

A nicely fitting skeet vest, with a sweater underneath should be ideal. Choose some comfortable footwear.

OTHER ITEMS

The remainder of your clothing is entirely up to you, but I am of the opinion that if your appearance is neat then your shooting is more likely to follow suit. If you look good, you feel good – and when you feel good you are half-way to achieving whatever is in your aim. Seriously, confidence plays a big part in all sports and especially in shooting. You have to go out there brimming with it.

Waterproofs

A useful buy is a pair of waterproofs from a sports shop, so that come rain or come shine, you are equipped. The advantage of waterproofs is that they give you protection from both the cold and the wet, without adding unnecessary inches onto your shoulder which would spoil your gun fit. They also give room for movement.

A set of nylon waterproofs will give sterling service in wet weather. They will cut out the cold and wet, but because they are thin they are unlikely to affect your gun mounting. Note also that sporting shot Pat Hennessy is wearing a pair of ear-muffs – it is essential that you wear some sort of hearing protection.

Headgear

As for headgear, I myself seldom wear any sort of hat, but that is a matter of personal preference. A shooting cap with a good brim to shield your eyes from the sun obviously makes sense.

Sunglasses

Sunglasses are another good investment. There are a number of coloured lenses on the market that help in different conditions. Certainly, some shooters seem to struggle to see blaze coloured targets properly, so a pair of red lenses would be of help here. Barry Simpson always wears Optix Cormorant glasses and is very pleased with them. They have the added advantage of being shot- and shatter-proof. Specialist trap shooters will need to find a pair of glasses with bigger lenses to accommodate the field of vision commanded by their chosen discipline. I would add again, that personally I avoid wearing any sort of glasses unless I am shooting into the glare of the sun. I feel it is best to remain uncluttered in any way, shape or form.

Gloves

A pair of good quality leather gloves or shooting mittens will help in deep mid-winter, and a sports or golf umbrella is always a useful aid. If you are lucky, you might be able to get hold of one at your local gunshop bearing the logo of your favourite gun or cartridge.

Shoe flap

Another item which might just fit into the clothing category is a shoe flap. This is a pear-shaped flat piece of leather which slots into your shoe laces and covers the front part of your foot. Its purpose is simply to enable you to rest your barrels on your shoe without leaving their calling card – two black circles!

Cartridge bag

You will also need a cartridge bag; the design and type is obviously down to personal preference. Another useful buy might be a cartridge magazine, so that you can simply lift out a box of sevens without sifting through countless nines! Or perhaps you might prefer to use a general sports bag for the same purpose. The latter is particularly useful as you can also carry with you your cleaning kit and a handy rag, plus your chosen form of hearing protection.

Ear-muffs

The need for some sort of hearing protection cannot be overstressed. Your ears can become badly damaged without you realising it is taking place – and sadly once your hearing starts to deteriorate there is no way that it can be restored. Again there is a good choice available, and I would recommend that you buy the best that you can afford; none are expensive. You might choose ear-muffs by Bilsom or Silenta or maybe some ear-plugs such as Gunfenders.

7 Competitions

As I mentioned earlier, the nice thing about clay pigeon shooting is that it can be cut according to the cloth. If your budget won't allow you to spend a lot of money on your sport (or for various reasons you want to restrict your expenditure) then the fortnightly or monthly club shoot will offer excellent value. But more likely than not, once you have got a taste for it then you will want to do more. You might join another club, or go along to a professional ground to shoot a round or two of practice. Let's be honest, once you have mastered the basics the only way to improve is to practise and practise. Shooting lots of cartridges won't make you a good shot in itself; you must at all times learn from your shooting. Even if it is only 'fun' practice, apply yourself properly and do everything correctly.

OPEN SHOOTS

After you have been a member of a club for a while it is likely that they will stage an 'open' shoot to raise money for club funds or perhaps a local charity. This will give you a good chance to measure your progress. It may be a thirty or forty sporting re-entry competition – re-entry meaning that you can enter as many times as you like. In theory this means that if you buy enough cards you will eventually return a perfect score. In some cases this is true – but don't bank on it. After a while it becomes apparent that no matter how much you invest on extra cards, you have difficulty in improving on your original score. Your best bet is to decide how much you are prepared to spend beforehand, and

then make every shot count. A couple of turns on the competition, and a further two cards for the pool shoot should account for £10. The pool shoot is a ten bird stand of going away or quartering birds which is normally run in conjunction with an open shoot. They are normally quite tricky and you tend not to get too many maximum 10ex10 scores.

The competition itself will be a real eye-opener. You will encounter something which you probably haven't felt since you first started – pressure! It doesn't matter that by now you know the club ground like the back of your hand, or that you have shot similar versions of the same stands several times before. In a competition, the targets are just one part of the problem – keeping your cool is the other!

Preparation

If it is your first competition, then you are stepping into the unknown. But that initial outing will show you that you really have to be in the right frame of mind to give your best.

Try and get in some extra practice beforehand. There are several clubs that shoot mid-week on summer evenings. A little extra practice could give you that extra edge of confidence.

Arrive at the shoot in good time and allow yourself plenty of time in which to shoot. Don't stipulate a given time by which you have to get your shooting completed. There could be problems, such as a big turn-out or a trap breakdown, and you would end up rushing the stands and returning an abysmal score.

Having shot practice at a local club or shooting ground, you will probably decide to have a go at a local open shoot.

When you get to the shoot, check out the stands to see what the targets are doing and how they are being shot. But be careful of this – no matter what you see, decide for yourself where you will break your targets using the style which has served you up until now.

Buy your cards, plan the order in which you will shoot the stands and don't leave it too late to get started.

Queuing

There is a degree of queuing involved in all open shoots. The sheer numbers attracted to them make it inevitable, and it is often impractical to have too many stands, which would either severely stretch manpower, or would mean you only shoot two or four birds per stand.

Queuing can be distracting but, like traffic jams, it must be endured. Use the time well by concentrating on the targets, so that when it comes to your turn you are pretty confident about their line of flight. But – bear in mind that they will look different from the point at which you shoot.

There are numerous problems which arise as a result of a twenty minute or longer wait to shoot your allotted birds. One of the chief of these is loss of concentration. You might get into a conversation with others awaiting their turn or, even worse, with someone who has just shot. The latter will probably give

57

Make good use of your queuing time. Look at the targets and be ready for when your name is called. Also make a point of not attempting to give your card to the referee when he is actually scoring.

you a lot of well-meant advice. Ignore it.

One of the great things about our sport is the friendliness. Everywhere you go it's the same – people always want a chat and they always want to help each other. So, by the time your card is called and you step onto the stand your concentration has gone, you were having a joke and a chat and you decide to shoot the targets like the chap who just got eight out of ten. You score three and you are not very happy! It's like having a bet: you know which horse you fancy, you have done your homework – but inspiration grabs you just minutes before the start and your bet goes on the horse which comes a gallant sixth, while your original choice romps home. Stick to your own chosen style.

Concentration

An important point to be learned from the above is to concentrate your mind on one thing only – shooting the targets the way you know best.

You will hear people say that they 'only shoot for fun', but they are hardly having fun when they walk off a stand having missed more than they hit. Conversely the world seems a much brighter and happier place altogether when you have put a good score together. So when it is within two or three guns of your turn, really switch into gear. Look at the targets, check that you have all the cartridges you need in your pocket (and two or three more besides) and think positive. When called you will be completely ready for the job in hand. You will think confident and be confident. Your style and swing will do the work for you and ten targets later you will be a very happy man indeed.

No birds

No birds are inevitable in any competition. Take them in your stride and don't let them unsettle your rhythm and confidence.

Under current rules if you get a pair of targets and one of them is a no bird, you will have to take both targets again (both kills to count). The fact that you hit the good bird on the first pair is irrelevant. So you should put that first pair completely out of your mind and concentrate totally on hitting both of the next. A common mistake is to take for granted the one you hit first time out and put all of your effort into the other bird. This is fatal. You will almost certainly miss the bird you are confident about.

This same attitude shows itself to a bigger extent on re-entry shoots. On your first card you might have done well on all except one stand. In theory if you have another card you should be able to put it all together – in practice you will often find that while you manage to crack the 'difficult' stand, you let much easier birds slip simply because you were blasé about them.

Another point worth remembering with no birds is not to rely totally on the support of the referee. It is amazing how quickly the mind works, and from the point of seeing the target you might notice it to be slightly off course and wait to hear a call of 'no bird'. Don't bank on it. If an experienced referee is in charge he will call the bird immediately – an inexperienced official, however, may not recognise that anything is wrong at all. So don't wait to hear the call. Be on your toes certainly and if the bird is obviously wrong

then put your gun down and request the bird again. But otherwise keep the momentum going and kill the target.

Varying targets

Varying targets can be a real problem with sporting shoots. Weather conditions obviously play a major role, and it can prove very difficult for a shoot organiser to keep his targets on a consistent line in a howling gale. Even a moderate wind or gust can play havoc. Likewise a change in wind direction during the shoot can alter the nature of the targets. The shoot organiser should be aware of this problem and make adjustments accordingly.

Similarly if the shoot organiser lacks experience it might be that he has not secured the traps properly, and their position will be prone to movement. This should be no concern of yours – there are bound to be many others who will be pointing it out to him in no uncertain manner. Don't get involved. You might only get steamed up and find yourself in a blazing row. It really isn't possible to shoot well after such an incident, so if you want to keep a cool and even equilibrium keep well out of the way. If, however, the trap suddenly moves while you are actually shooting, you can quietly point the fact out to the scorer and suggest in the nicest way possible that the trap be checked. But don't make a big scene of it.

Excuses

We all have our 'off' days. As much of your competitive shooting will be dependent on your mental attitude, there are bound to be those occasions when the biorhythms are not working for you! But for goodness' sake don't start bleating a string of excuses as to why you didn't do well. Everyone has their own problems and the last thing they want to hear are your excuses.

The next time you go to shoot make a point of listening for them – bad trappers, blind scorers, wrong gun, wrong cartridge, shot into the sun – the list is endless. But if you look at the scores you will see that somebody won the shoot, and probably with a high score. There will be other good scores too, so obviously they didn't find it a problem. For some people moaning is part and parcel of their day's shooting. Personally, I think it is something that the sport could well do without.

On the other hand, you can get a lot of pleasure talking about the stands with pals afterwards; how you tackled a certain target, how you missed or hit it and which you enjoyed the most. You will find that everyone will be doing that anyway – and also wishing that they could have another crack at the one which let them down.

Safety

This should come at the top of every chapter, but unfortunately it can make tedious reading so I'll include it wherever I can.

Don't forget to be safe at all times. It doesn't matter how well you shoot as long as you do it safely. Remember – keep your gun unloaded and broken at all times other than when you are on the stand waiting to shoot. When you load your gun lift the wood to the metal, i.e. move the stock rather than the barrels.

If you have to turn to speak to the referee, break your gun before doing so; and at all times keep a loaded gun pointing towards the range. If on any occasion you might be considered unsafe and someone points it out to you, don't argue – simply be grateful. Remember – guns are made to kill.

Consideration

While waiting your turn on a sporting shoot don't start laughing and joking at the top of your voice. Think of the man who is about to take his shot. While we all try to lock ourselves into a world where there is just us and the target, a raucous laugh or someone talking loudly at a key point can easily penetrate that concentration barrier.

Also, of course, be considerate to yourself! Don't carry a conversation on into the shooting station; and after you have had two or three shots don't turn round and make some kind of comment to anyone who happens to be at hand. You find yourself doing this without realising it – it helps to release the tension and introduce a degree of flippancy into your shooting. Forget it! Whether you have just hit the clays or missed them, it is nothing to do with anyone else. You have practised and trained towards a competition and you would be letting yourself down to think about anything other than breaking the next targets to appear.

Scorecards

There are two or three points to remember with scorecards. Firstly, make sure that you look after your own card properly; keep it in a pocket where it isn't screwed up or likely to get dirty, wet or defaced. Hand it to the scorer at a convenient point, not when he is actually in the process of marking someone else's card. When you hand it in make a mental note of approximately how many cards there are to be shot before yours comes to the top. After you have shot, check your score to make sure that it has been added up correctly. It won't take a second but it will save you a tremendous amount of hassle later – the scorer will never remember your particular card amongst countless others, so if there is a discrepancy it should be pointed out immediately.

Again I would emphasise, don't go losing your temper. We are all human and all fallible – if you ever do any scoring (and if you are a member of club no doubt your turn has already come) you will know how easy it is to mark K instead of L, or X instead of O. So point out politely the offending error and it will probably be corrected without any fuss.

The real problem occurs on the rare occasion when you and the referee are in disagreement. You say you chipped a bit off the bird – he says you missed it. Maybe other shooters who had been watching will come to your rescue. Though really the referee would be perfectly correct to stick to what he said – he can only score what he actually saw. The influential factor here is bias. We see what we like to see – we can't help it, this is the way we are made. The referee, however, has nothing at stake other than to do his job properly. So as I said earlier, don't get all steamed up about it – if he is adamant that you missed then his decision will stand. If that lost target will have a significant bearing on the competition, then perhaps you might take the complaint further. Though I personally would only do this under extreme circumstances. It usually just isn't worth the hassle.

The final and most important part about

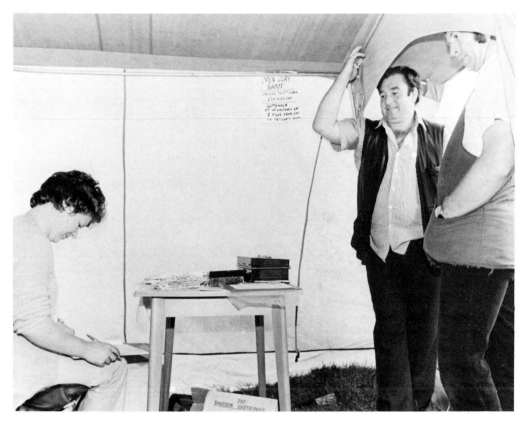

Return your card to the entry tent as soon as possible – and resist the temptation of checking your placing every few minutes!

scorecards is to always hand your card in to the entry office as soon as it is complete. Some people simply forget and leave them in their pockets, others feel that their score isn't worth returning and I think there are one or two who, for some unknown reason, prefer to hold onto them right until the very end. But if you want to do everyone a favour, yourself included, return the card as soon as possible. The office staff will have been working hard all day and the end of the shoot is always a messy task. Inevitably there will be a rush of completed cards and everyone wants their placings at once. But it is impossible for the office staff to work out placings until they know that all the cards have been returned. If there are empty spaces on their check list they don't know if someone is still shooting or whether he has gone home. So always return your card.

Having returned your card, don't be one of those people who keep pestering the office to see where they have finished. I know that it's tempting if you have put a good score in – you are thrilled by your efforts and you can't wait for the outcome. But with a little patience, you will find out soon enough.

BIGGER COMPETITIONS

Having entered one or two local open shoots you will discover the pleasure and challenge of sporting competition. It puts an added edge on your shooting and even though your scores might be down on practice, you find that it offers tremendous stimulation. There is always an atmosphere about an open shoot: it is infectious; it induces nerves, gets the adrenalin flowing and can do all sorts of funny things to your shooting. But if you can channel it in your favour then you can easily surprise yourself. So what is the next step?

Clay Pigeon Shooting Association

I would advise anyone taking up clay pigeon shooting to join the Clay Pigeon Shooting Association. Commonly known as the CPSA, membership is a nominal £10 per annum which gives you insurance liability to £1 million, and offers eligibility to the big registered competitions and your name in the classification lists. Through regional committees the CPSA runs a variety of area and county championships for all the disciplines, and two big championships for each discipline, the British Open and English Open (in the case of the international disciplines these are the British and English Grand Prix).

In addition to the area and county championships you will find that your better local grounds will also run registered shoots. This means that your scores at such events (and the championships) will be returned to the CPSA headquarters in Epping where they will be fed into a computer.

Classifications

There are four classifications, and score averages are published twice yearly so that you can enter a class at any of the shoots mentioned above. For sporting, the relevant qualifying scores are AA, A, B, C. There are also ladies', juniors' (under eighteen) and veterans' classes.

The great advantage of this system over the open shoot is that while the open event offers tremendous competitive practice, for the beginner there is not much chance of actually winning anything. With the classification system however, if you join the CPSA on taking up the sport (or soon after) you will probably see your name appearing in Class C in the first relevant averages book.

The prizes in all of the classes are comparable. In fact, if there are more C shooters at an event than others, you may find that this class will offer a better payout. Whatever, there will be a minimum thirty per cent payout at all registered shoots.

As you progress, you will make your way through the classes. To reach AA you need to be of a very high standard, but it is surprising what practice and experience can do for your shooting – especially if you always do everything properly and never forget stance, mounting and style.

Planning your shoots

Many of these championships are 100 bird events so naturally the cost of taking part is higher. At the time of writing, entry fees were in the £18 region. Add to this the cost of your cartridges, travel and in some cases, accommodation, and clearly they are not cheap. But if you plan your expenditure properly you will find that there is some terrific pleasure to be enjoyed. For a start I feel that it is always a good idea to find a friend of comparable ability so that the two of you can do your shooting together. This helps in many ways. You can plan your shooting, share the cost of travel and help each other at the actual events. You want to be sure that you are equally keen and then you will find that each other's enthusiasm is infectious.

It is a lot of fun sorting out your diary so that you know which shoots to take in and which to avoid. If you want to do maybe one or two big ones I would always recommend the British or English, no matter where they are. You really get the sense of occasion; there is a buzz in the air and a thrill to be had from actually taking part. Travelling together will give an added pleasure. You will have looked forward to the big day and hopes will be high.

At the shoot, it might not go as well as

planned. But having a friend means that you can cheer each other up. One bad stand isn't the end of the world in a hundred bird shoot – you can soon make up a bit of leeway. Encouraging each other will bring out the best in both of you. At the end of the day, whatever the result, you have enjoyed it; and no doubt you will shoot all those targets time and time again on the journey home. It is an amusing thought that every Sunday evening there are cars travelling our roads countrywide holding clay shoot inquests. 'If only . . . it was the third stand . . . you shot it well . . . I'm having trouble with teal birds . . .' and so on. Great, isn't it!

Scoreboards

Scoreboards hold an irresistible magic. At any shoot, anywhere, you will always see people gathered around them. Everyone wants to know how everyone else got on, who did well, who didn't and what sort of scores they've got to beat. That last part is the deadly aspect of it all. Never forget that you can do nothing about anyone else's score but you can do everything about your own. So disregard any scores that have come in or you'll start calculating how many you need to get a place – or how many you can afford to drop. This can work for some people; it adds to their determination if they are in sight of somebody they would very much like to beat. But it can also backfire; it can easily introduce a negative aspect to your round. You might talk yourself out of the possibility of achieving a decent placing, or maybe by calculating how many misses you can afford you sell yourself short in terms of performance.

The only person that you really have to beat is yourself. Shoot each and every target as though it is the only one that counts. Don't think in terms of your overall score, or even of shooting half of the stands well. Simply concentrate on one target at a time – take care of the pennies and the pounds look after themselves. It's an old adage but it makes a lot of sense.

Of course, it is only natural to feel good when you have shot and killed the first three pairs of a stand (virtually all hundred bird shoots will comprise ten stands of ten birds). The flaw is to think about ten straight – never contemplate anything further than the very next clay. This is the only one that counts every time. Letting your concentration wander to other things is letting your score go adrift. So ignore the scoreboard and surprise yourself.

Pressure

The real leveller in big competitions is pressure. Can you handle it? You will see shots at your local club who look absolutely unbeatable. It amazes you that they don't enter any of the major contests – they would be sure to win. Or would they? The chances are that they have tried one or two big competitions in the past only to produce a bitterly disappointing score. Their score might have been decent, but nothing like they would have shot against similar targets at the local club. The simple reason is that the heat can get a little high in the atmosphere of a major championship.

So take heart. Adopt a positive approach. You have nothing at stake and, contrary to what you might think, your score is of no consequence to anyone except yourself. Nobody is watching how you perform and if you were to step off a stand probably only the scorer would know how many you had scored. So ignore the people standing behind you; there is only you, the gun and the clay.

Keep your cool, check your foot position, the point at which you will aim your muzzles and the point at which you will kill the targets. When you are totally ready and feel confident that you can swing and shoot that first target call 'Pull'. (Another point here incidentally, make sure that you know the appropriate 'ready' word – it could be pull, mark or ready.) After you have killed the first target your confidence will start to flow. Keep it flowing, but just keep telling yourself 'one target at a time'. Sorry to labour that point, but it is so important.

Stand sequence

With ten stands to shoot, you obviously have to decide a sequence which you feel will help. I believe there are one or two shoots now which are insisting that stands be taken in a certain order. Whether that is right or wrong, it certainly removes one of the decisions from the permutation.

The sequence you decide on is probably a matter of personal preference and which stands you feel the most confident about. Some people prefer to shoot the stands regardless of difficulty but in order of the length of queues. Some stands may have long queues – others will be through in no time. You will notice that those stands with the longer queues are those with on report targets. Doubles are shot much more quickly.

Some like to start on relatively straightforward targets, building up to the more difficult ones to be taken around half to two-thirds of the way through. By that time you will have built up a rhythm and your confidence. Then you can finish downhill on straightforward targets. Leaving a difficult stand until last should be avoided. You might have built a mental block about it and talked yourself out of getting a decent score. If you have your friend with you, then between the two of you a decent sequence can be planned. But whatever you do, don't start building the harder stands up out of all proportion.

Some people like to loose off a few shells at the pool stand before they start. I have mixed views about this. While in theory the idea of getting loosened up is sound, in practice the pool stand is often very difficult and can have the effect of sowing a few seeds of doubt about your ability. Dropping six targets on the pool stand is hardly going to put you in the best frame of mind before you start. It would be better to pick a nice straightforward stand on the competition course to get you into the groove. When your hundred birds are completed you can blast away at the pool to your heart's content!

Arrive at the ground in good time. Give yourself time to wind down, maybe have a cup of tea, then walk round the course looking at the different stands in turn. Check the flight lines, the types of target (is it a long distance standard clay or a closer midi?) and the likely position of the sun and wind. When you feel you are totally ready, start – but don't leave it too late or you'll find yourself rushing to finish. Give yourself time to enjoy the shoot and ample opportunity to get the kind of score you were hoping for.

Shoot-offs

Now we are really talking about pressure. In fact, that is all we are talking about, for if you find your way into a shoot-off you have already beaten most of the entries or most of your class so you know that your shooting is up to it.

The shoot-off is the showcase finale to the whole event, and while it often means that it will add more time onto the end of a shoot, a major competition without a shoot-off is never quite the same. Hopefully, as many competitors as possible will have waited to the end. Certainly if it is a big competition then there will be quite a crowd by virtue of the fact that all the class prize winners will be present.

In CPSA competitions one of the existing stands is selected (see rules). But other organisers may opt for a completely new stand or two of the stands on the course (maybe with the targets slightly altered). I enjoy, if possible, putting on something completely different at my ground, preferably in the shape of fifteen to twenty birds using three or four traps. This may sound like a lot of fuss. But if it is a big competition, I believe that it should hang on much more than a straightforward repeat of ten targets that have already been shot by all parties. Another option is sudden death – miss a target and you are out of it.

Whatever sort of shoot-off you find yourself in simply make all the usual checks. Have a good look at the targets and if you feel confident (and there is every reason that you must!) and you are given the option, elect to go first. This advice might sound a little odd, but if you step forward and shoot to the best of your ability you will get a good score and in the process you will put the pressure on your opponent.

If you are not confident about the target when shown one by the referee, then you can put the other man on the spot and watch the clays carefully so that you know exactly what to do when it is your turn. But whenever you shoot (and the decision may be taken by the shoot-off organiser), lock yourself away from all that is going on around you, ignore any advice that is given and simply get out there and do the business. Let the other man do all the worrying.

Win or lose – be a gentleman. Shake hands, being neither too elated nor too despondent – if the other man has lost he doesn't want to see you gloating, and if he has won then you must do yourself justice and show dignity in defeat.

The shoot-off is always an exciting climax to any shoot – and you have to be able to handle pressure. International sporting shot John Bidwell is ignoring all that is going on behind him and simply concentrating on breaking the targets.

Presentations

It is always nice if as many people as possible can stay to the end of a shoot for the presentations. I know that it is difficult in many cases where long journeys are involved, but those able to stay should be there at the end. This is particularly the case in sponsored events. Too often in the past companies have given very welcome sponsorship to the sport but felt that it was never properly appreciated. If shooting is to move forward then it needs all the outside help it can get.

FEMALE COMPETITORS

I would like to take this opportunity to stress that each part of this book is equally applicable to women as it is to men. There are no special instructional details because when it comes to shooting, physique is of little consequence. There is no reason why women cannot shoot every bit as well as men, providing they follow all the basic guidelines of gun fit, stance, mounting and method.

We have some great female shots in this country. Anthea Hillyer is a perfect example, she holds her ground with almost anyone. There is now a growing number of women in the sport, but even so they are very much in the minority and often feel that people are paying undue attention to them when they are shooting. But, the same as for the men, when you are about to shoot, just concentrate on those targets and forget the rest.

COLTS

The real problem for young shots is one of finance; with a limited income shooting can clearly be a problem. But somehow or other there are lots of youngsters overcoming it and shooting tremendously well. This is, of course, the time to start; the eyes and senses are sharp and the brain is used to the learning process and has a capacity to absorb instruc-

tion. What often happens, however, is that teenagers take up shooting, make good progress and then drift off for one reason or another. Often they come back to it though, and they soon find that they pick it up again quite quickly, having properly learned the basics.

Again, there is no specific advice for colts, other than to get onto a 12-bore as soon as possible. An interesting point about young shooters is that their progress is much more rapid. Rather than being overpowered by an occasion, they are often fearless and wade straight in to return good scores. It is tremendous to see young lads shooting well, and it obviously gives a lot of pride to their parents.

No matter how big or small the shoot, it is always nice if as many people as possible stay on to the end for the presentations.

There is nothing like getting into good shooting habits at an early age –
this is when pupils are the most receptive to instruction.

REPRESENTATIVE SHOOTING

There is no greater honour in any sport than to represent one's country. In all of the domestic disciplines, you have the opportunity to win your way through to represent your country in international competitions, which are hosted by England, Scotland, Ireland and Wales in turn. The selection procedures vary but basically the honour is within the reach of everyone who takes part in clay shooting providing they have both the ability and commitment. All shooters are selected on merit. Taking it a step further, the international disciplines of FITASC Sporting, Olympic trap, ISU skeet and Universal trench all have representative teams taking part in the major European and World Championships.

What could be finer than to be selected to represent your country on some of the finest shooting grounds in the world? Maybe only one thing – the Olympics. Both Olympic trap and ISU skeet are recognised Olympic sports and Britain sends teams for both disciplines to the Olympic Games. Bob Braithwaite's gold medal was one of Britain's few successes in the Mexico Olympics of 1968. So stick at it! The world of clay competition is literally at your fingertips.

8 Forty English Sporting

To put theory into practice let's look at shooting a typical round of 40 sporting. In fact, it is not entirely typical, for while the stands depicted will feature in some way or other in most sporting competitions, for the purposes of simplicity of illustration they all have doubles. In reality the major competitions will mix the targets, with doubles (as shown), on report or stand combinations. The same rules apply however, always remembering to get yourself into the correct position. Your front foot (left for right-hander) will be pointed in the direction at which you will break the clay, and it will also be carrying the weight.

TEAL

Teal is a target with which many people have problems. The most common reason for error is that they start with the gun too low. You must remember that on a sporting lay-out most targets will have been in flight before you see them and they are travelling at their fastest during the first ten yards. If you aim towards the top of the trap you'll go racing after the target at 100 miles per hour (particularly if it is a single, which travels half as fast again as a double).

Some people also use a trap gun. This again causes problems if they have been using their sporter on all the other stands, though I'll admit the teal is a stand that is well suited to 30 inch barrels. However, I would always stick to my 27½ inch gun, the one I am familiar with. I have often used skeet shells for this stand but it is perhaps most sensible to use trap cartridges. So definitely use a

seven for the second bird and maybe for both.

Start with your muzzle up, so that when you mount on to the target it will be at least five yards or so in the air. You will track the first bird (go for the straighter bird) move through and kill – this will be just over half-way up to the peak of its flight. Then move onto the second bird and kill just before it reaches the top.

If it's a single clay you will follow the same procedure but as it is travelling faster you will take it at about two-thirds to three-quarters of the way up, or maybe even nearer the top.

Remember – hold your gun up and look over the muzzles for the point at which you will mount.

OVERHEAD

The overhead target, often described as either pigeon or duck, is the one that breaks all the rules – you start on the back foot and you track the target in front! Let me explain.

The trap will be situated behind you so you will want to have a look at the flight of the targets as you get ready to mount. Therefore, to look backwards slightly you must go onto your back foot, holding the gun sharply upwards. If you wait until the bird is directly over you or in front it is fairly certain that you will flash at it and also pretty likely that you will miss.

It is often a good idea to use a skeet shell in the first barrel and a trap in the second. Cartridge choice on this stand all depends on the speed and height of the targets in question,

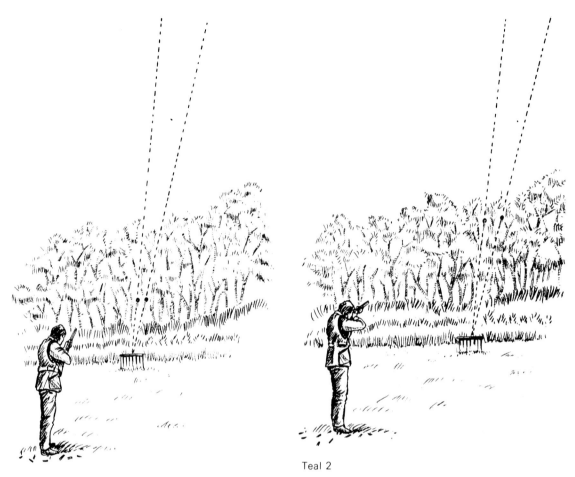

Teal 1

Teal 2

but it may be that the second clay will be well out away from you before you can shoot at it. So go on your back foot, looking slightly back call the target and as it (or they) come into view move onto your front foot and mount the gun with the muzzles on the front edge of the clay. It has to be the front (as opposed to back edge) or you simply wouldn't see it, and you can't follow something you can't see!

If it is a pair, again go for the straighter of the two – this will give you more time for the more difficult wider bird. There is obviously no definite place at which I can advise taking the targets, other than what is the simplest and the one that fits into your rhythm. But don't leave it too late – it will get much more difficult.

The first bird can often be likened to high house skeet – but it can also be quite different. Have a good look at others shooting it, and decide for yourself the most sensible killing points.

Take the single teal towards the peak of its flight – but don't leave it too long.

Teal 3

TOWER

I think it is fair to say that most people enjoy shooting a tower. Yet despite this you often see targets missed – sometimes rather a lot of them! This is because the guns either read the target wrongly or fail to follow their normal shooting pattern.

Almost regardless of height, I shoot tower birds with skeet cartridges. But before getting onto a stand you should make sure that you can follow the full line of flight and

establish whether the bird is a midi or a normal. If your flight judgement is wrong you will shoot up the side of the target (mostly because of bad mounting), and if it is a midi it will not be as high as it appears, but travelling faster. That might be stating the obvious but this is just what happens.

Also, remember the same instruction as the teal, don't start with your muzzles aiming at a point close to the trap. If you look at *Tower 1* you will see that my gun is being held at a point above the trees, giving the clay

an opportunity of steadying its speed and getting clear into the sky.

Go for the straighter bird first, pick it up, track it and swing through. I like to take the bird just in front – you might find, however, that you can shoot with greater confidence when it is directly above you. The only shortcoming of this arises when you have a close pair. If you shoot the first at ninety degrees you will obviously struggle with the second. Alternatively if the second bird is a wide one, don't forget to move your feet; if you attempt to simply twist your body the gun stock will almost certainly come off your face and the bird will be lost. Don't consider taking birds behind you as going away targets. This is a dangerous practice which most referees frown upon – in any event a cage, or some other restricting factor, should be provided.

Remember – while your tracking will tell you the correct line of flight and target speed and therefore dictate the amount of lead, you

Overhead 1

Overhead 2

Overhead 3

must keep that gun moving; stop the gun when you squeeze the trigger and you will miss it behind!

WOODCOCK

The woodcock is a target on which all your practice at mounting and style will come into its own. You will see this bird at certain grounds flash through trees - and similarly you will see guns flash and miss. If you don't do everything properly it can be a very difficult target - if you simply follow all the correct procedure you will be amazed at how straightforward it can be. I would use skeet shells for woodcock, every time. It is, in fact, a sharp flat skeet target and the use of trap shells is inappropriate.

Having watched others shoot the stand you will know exactly the line of flight and where you intend to take the birds. Get in position, with your foot towards the point of

Overhead pair - remember, back bird first.

73

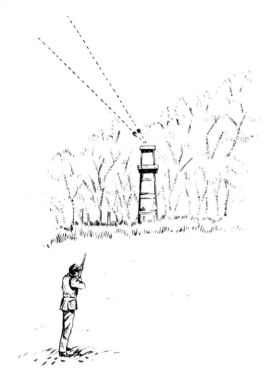

Tower 1

Tower 3

Tower 2

the kill and the gun muzzles brought back to line up ready for the flight of the clay as soon as it comes into view. When you are ready, call 'Mark' (always make sure you know the required 'ready' word.).

You will really want your wits about you (as with all clays) and you will need to pick the bird, mount, track and swing through with great fluidity. Don't panic, and don't worry about not having enough time – if you have been concentrating on getting your approach work right it will serve you well.

The other important point to remember is that if you are shooting at two clays on this stand (as illustrated), take the back bird first. Some might think it best to take the front bird first so that the back bird isn't so far away when you shoot. This is wrong – if you shoot the front bird, you will inevitably check your swing to get onto the one that is

Woodcock 1

Woodcock 2

Woodcock 3

following it. On the other hand, by taking the back bird you will automatically follow your swing through onto the front one and be able to take it with a minimum of fuss.

At Mid-Norfolk we often couple a single woodcock (again much faster than a double) with a tower bird, which is thrown on report. The procedure is a simple translation of the instruction for the two stands. If you are required to take the woodcock first, concentrate on it and nothing else – the other bird cannot be released until you have fired. On shooting, immediately dismiss any thoughts of whether you have killed or lost the target and quickly transfer your foot to the neces-

sary point, coolly going through the correct sequence to take the tower bird. For goodness' sake don't panic, you will always have time – just collect yourself and do it properly.

As with all stands don't worry about what is going on behind you – and don't get involved with any banter that may be offered. If it is clear that you are concentrating on the job in hand the referee will come to your aid and tell everyone to quieten down. Neither rush your shooting nor take too long about it. Think positive and form a nice steady pattern for taking the ten birds on each stand. Shooting is all about getting into good habits.

9 FITASC Sporting

The discipline commonly known as FITASC Sporting, would really be more appropriately titled International Sporting. FITASC is the abbreviated title of the ruling body, *Federation Internationale de Tir aux Armes Sportives de Chasse*, who also have the responsibility for Universal Trench (5-trap). So what is FITASC Sporting and how does it differ from English sporting?

LAYOUT

From the illustrations of a typical Norfolk layout (overleaf) I hope you will be able to see the difference to the homespun variety. The essential criterion is that no two targets shot by any individual will be alike. In other words, it is as near to game shooting as possible, and every target is a new and fresh challenge. That is what gives it such terrific appeal. Imagination should play a strong role in devising a course using a wide range of traps, speeds and angles, plus the different clays – normal, midi, mini, battue and rabbit. There is another clay called the rocket which is used on the Continent but really has nothing to offer that cannot be achieved by the five I have mentioned.

There are three different stands from which the competitor will complete his twenty-five targets. Each layout (twenty-five targets) will be shot by a squad of six guns at an allotted time. Because of the high number of trappers and equipment involved, you can't rattle through the entries like five doubles on English Sporting. A 150 bird competition will normally be held over two days, and a 200 bird international championship will take three to four days. I held a one-day event over 100 targets at Mid-Norfolk Shooting School last year. We were oversubscribed and it ran rather late, but properly planned it is certainly possible to put 72 guns through in a day for such an event. Of course, the extra manpower and lower number of participants inevitably means that FITASC is a much more expensive discipline to stage. But by and large you find that shooters (and I include myself) don't mind paying a little bit more for what is a superb form of shotgun shooting.

METHOD

All the same principles apply to FITASC as to English sporting. During the last couple of years the winning scores have been incredibly high: A. J. Smith, for instance, won his European title with 190 and even in the difficult World Championship in South Africa Gerry Cowler produced a winning score of 183. These are scores that would probably not be achieved in an English sporting competition. What FITASC gives the shooter is the added edge. The top shooters will excel because they have mastered the principles of good shooting. Because each target is different, the approach work must be right first time on every occasion. Gerry and A. J. are good examples. They shoot FITASC extremely well yet have never won a major English sporting title. I am sure that if you checked their scorecards you would find that in English sporting the dropped targets are in the second half of the ten birds on the offending stands. A. J. in particular

THE SEQUENCE FOR THE NORFOLK LAYOUT

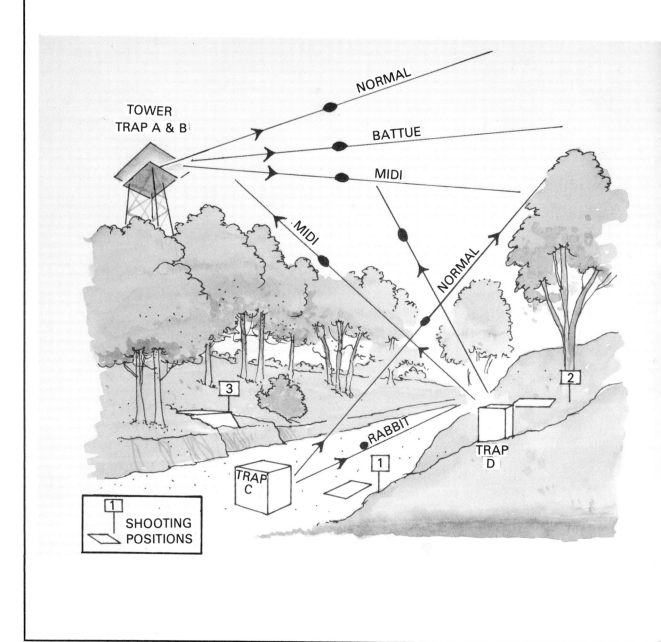

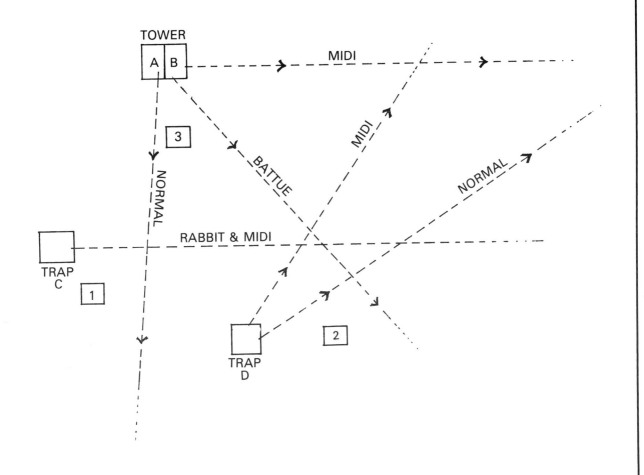

Stand One: Singles – A normal clay; C normal; D midi; B midi.
              Doubles – A normal plus D midi; C normal plus B midi.
Stand Two: Singles – B battue; C rabbit; D normal; A normal; C normal.
              Doubles – B battue; C normal plus D normal; C rabbit plus A
              normal.
Stand Three: Singles – A normal; C rabbit; B midi; D normal.
              Doubles – B midi plus C rabbit; D normal plus A normal.
Total: 25 targets.

The 1985 FITASC Sporting World Championship at Wynyard Park, Cleveland. Keith Blockley (Bronze medallist) is taking a right to left rabbit. If you look above the shooters' heads you will see another trap house and a further one at the top right of the picture. The traps are used in a variety of sequences so that shooting from different positions, each competitor never shoots the same kind of target twice.

will be the first to admit that it is the simplest birds that cost him his British and English aspirations. The concentration probably drifts after hitting the first of a couple of straightforward pairs – in FITASC, however, with each target being different this never happens.

Reading a target, approach work and consistently smooth and fluid mounting and swing will take you anywhere, and in FITASC they can bring extremely satisfying dividends.

If you look at the diagram, you will see the lines of flight from the three tower birds. If you were queuing and chatting away at a regular sporting competition you might not notice much difference between these birds, even if they were all the same type of target. But they each demand a different approach. Add to the equation that in this instance I would throw a normal, midi and battue and

you really have a different proposition. Midis are an extremely deceptive target. Smaller (at 90mm) than the standard clay, they often appear at first glance to be higher than they actually are. The reason for this, of course, is their size. They also fly faster. The battue can be a real brute. It doesn't have the lip of a normal clay and as a consequence tends to twist in flight.

The clays shown will all keep a consistent line of flight, and by using the three different shooting positions the shooter will be getting his full variety. The different nature of all the shots is the source of satisfaction in their taking; and while prize money is always nice, FITASC Sporting really is a sport in which the true pleasure comes from pitting your own ability against each and every target. Yes, not so much the winning, but the taking part.

10 Sporting Variations

THE TOWER

The tower bird is not only an enjoyable stand to shoot, it also highlights strengths and weaknesses in technique. If a shoot features a high tower bird there is a good likelihood that it will attract a decent entry. Though more grounds are now equipping themselves with a tower, their cost is such that the average club simply cannot justify the investment.

Consequently, when many guns enter their area or county championship, or even the British or English, they are getting a rare taste of a target which might bemuse them. Some step forward and shoot it with the greatest of ease; others struggle badly and rely chiefly on friends to tell them how much lead they should be giving the target. This, of course, is nonsense. Depending on the speed of thought process and the style of shooting, any given target can demand lead varying from nothing to six feet. So ignore any offers of assistance, no matter how well meant, and shoot the stand with your own tried and trusted method. Listen politely to advice given (to avoid appearing either conceited or ungrateful) but put it clean out of your head when it comes to shooting.

Using your own method (which I have described) the tower bird calls for straight-forward sighting, tracking, mounting, swing and shoot (still keeping that gun swinging). Examine the following photographs and see the various ways in which it is possible to shoot tower birds.

Tower 1

Oooops! Just about everything wrong here. The gun is off the face, the shot is taken too far back, off the back foot – and it all boils down to one thing. The stance was wrong when the bird was called.

If you look at the front (left) foot you will see that the toe is pointing somewhere in the region of 2 o'clock in relation to the target. (The right foot should have been pointing in that direction). Consequently the whole of the body is at an angle to the target's flight, resulting in the shooter having to twist round to take his shot. As he went back his gun would almost certainly have moved off his face, and his shot therefore could have gone virtually anywhere in the sky.

Moreover by shooting as late as this he was making the target very difficult for himself. A high bird, once it has lost its speed and direction, is a very awkward target to come to terms with.

Tower 2

That's better. The shooter is straining a little, but essentially he has got it right. The body is facing forward to the direction from which the target has travelled, the weight is on the front foot and the shot is being taken on the swing through.

My only qualms about this one are that, if anything, the shooter is leaving it a little late to take his shot. But it may have been a very high target, in which case he is perfectly correct in taking it directly overhead.

Tower 1

Tower 2

Tower 3

Tower 4

Tower 5

Tower 3

There's more than one way of skinning a cat –
Brian Hebditch is pictured here shooting a
tower bird sideways on, almost as if it were a
crosser. Brian is one of our best shots and his
ability enables him to take targets in this
manner. But any shooter with less experience
would be stacking the odds against himself.
By turning sideways you are increasing the
margin of error, for by twisting back to pick
up the target's flight you are making it harder
to stick to your tried and trusted method of
shooting.

Also, it is certainly very much more
difficult to track a target in this way. You can
swing the gun either side of it as well as
making yourself more prone to pulling the
gun off the face. Extreme right angle birds
can be very hard if you don't have a good
shooting position. Taken facing the tower,
however, you merely have to pick up the line
of the bird as it flies over you.

Tower 4

Here is another example of bad positioning.
The front foot was obviously pointing to the
right of the tower as the bird was called. The
overhead bird is swinging slightly to the left
of the shooter, who has unwittingly dropped
his right shoulder to track it round. The
dropping of the shoulder is invariably a
direct result of bad positioning of the feet.
Needless to say, while it is still possible to hit
a target from such a stance, this is a very
difficult way of doing it!

Tower 5

The clay is in the air, but I'll put my money
on it being broken. The style is good:
relaxed, weight on the front foot (which is
pointing at the target), the gun is nicely
mounted and the shooter is correctly tracking the target before swinging through and
smashing it.

Tower 6

The same shooter tackles a right-handed tower bird. His position is good and he is shown moving in behind to track it. In his sight picture a small gap will appear between his muzzles and the clay.

When he is confident of the speed and the line he will swing smoothly through and break it. The temptation on this bird is to jerk in front of the clay – this should obviously be resisted, and gun movement must be kept smooth and even at all times.

Tower 7

A pair of clays from a low tower; note the posts and the string across the top to stop the shooter from taking targets beyond ninety degrees. As a left-hander the gun is probably wise to take the wider right-hand bird first; it might be tricky for him to swing onto a low fast bird such as this with his second barrel. But any right-handed competitor would, on a stand such as this, take the more straight-forward oncomer with his first shot, to give him time to get onto the right-hander.

If this was a high tower stand with very much higher birds of similar direction, I would also recommend that left-handed shots should take the straight bird first, then quickly adjust the foot position and shoot the right-hand bird.

Tower 6

Tower 7

BOLTING RABBIT

There are very many shots who come un-stuck on this target. The fact that they have to shoot a moving target on the ground within a given (usually quite short) distance completely throws them. Pointing the gun downwards tends to have two effects – it stops barrel swing and causes people to shoot over the top of the target.

As you wait for your turn to shoot, simply think in terms of a straightforward crosser. The speed might be off-putting, whether it is very fast or very slow you tend to think too much about it and endeavour to be precise with the shot. This, of course, results in a miss behind.

Shooting over the top is an unusual phen-omenon, peculiar to DTL and bolting rabbit. I know the reason for swinging through a levelling trap target, but the bolting rabbit has me mystified. I can only assume that people are concerned about shooting at the ground. Something in their mind tells them to keep their gun up. If, however, you simply follow the usual procedure of position, stance, mounting and tracking you'll break a rabbit nine times out of ten. Ignore the ground on which it is travelling.

Rabbit 1

This chap has almost everything right, but highlights the point I make above! He is going for precision, has stopped his gun movement and is shooting over the top. The style is good though and he will probably kick himself, before getting it right with his next shot.

Rabbit 2

The rabbit is a popular feature of major international FITASC Sporting shoots, and as you will notice they tend not to do the shooter any favours! You will note that there is only the smallest of gaps during which the target will show itself; but the competitor in question will have picked up its speed and trajectory from the first gap (look beyond the area in front of the man seated). The style is good, note the foot position pointing to the direction at which the shot is taken. The rabbit is reduced to a cloud of smoke.

Rabbit 3

There is one other problem with clay rabbits – they tend to fly! This can be a little disconcerting, but don't worry about it too much. If you track the bird as normal, this is a quick shot and your swing will mostly go

Rabbit 1

Rabbit 2

Rabbit 3

Quartering 1

with it. You will find that 'flying' rabbits are more common at local shoots – major competitions will feature more standardised targets.

QUARTERING

Quartering targets are those which are both going away and also angled across the shooter – this can be from his right and left, and from almost any conceivable position.

Quartering 1

This is a good example of a quartering pair. It is a fairly straightforward shot, but made to appear slightly more difficult due to the fact that there are two targets.

You will note that on this particular stand, the waiting shots have a good view of the flight of the clays. So you would be well advised to make good use of your queuing time, making a particular note during the period immediately before your turn. By doing this, you will see that the best way of shooting the targets is to take the back target first (as in the photograph) before swinging onto the next target. Don't leave the shot too long as this kind of target can soon start to drop and there is a fair chance you'll go over the top of the second one.

Quartering 2

This snipe stand looks a fairly tricky proposition, but don't talk yourself out of hitting the target. Adopt a positive attitude and observe the targets carefully and also how the better shots take the birds.

One thing to remember on a quartering stand where the trap is situated adjacent to your shooting peg (as I suspect this one is), is that the first ten yards of the target's flight will be its fastest, so don't pull your gun back too far. There is no other special rule other than to follow your good shooting code – stance, mount, track and kill the target, not forgetting to keep those barrels moving.

Quartering 3

This is a variation on the quartering stand which we like to feature at Mid-Norfolk. Many guns have problems with it, yet given the usual thought and respect it is not really as difficult as it seems.

The target depicted is flying on a low trajectory from left to right. As with the rabbit, the most common fault when pointing a gun downwards is to use it like a rifle, and an aimed rifle tends not to move much! In other words, most people shoot behind. On top of this, again like the rabbit, it is also easy to miss over the target.

You must try to put the background completely out of your mind, especially the fact that you are shooting downwards; just think in terms of you and the clay. Don't forget either to keep those barrels moving. You will also note that if this particular shot is left too late there is an obstruction (in the shape of a tree) which also psychologically tells you to stop the swing of your gun.

Quartering 2

Quartering 4

Another quartering pair; this time they are being released from a trap in front and to the left of the shooter. The pair leave the trap quickly, rising only marginally before dropping over the bank.

This particular shooter has let his weight drop onto his back foot with the consequence that he has swung through the birds and gone straight over the top of them. As they dip when losing speed over the bank, his swing has obviously followed their immediate trajectory. In fact, if this chap had got his weight forward, he wouldn't have been quite so hunched when he took the shot. His foot position is quite good and he is endeavouring to take the clays at the correct point. Taken off the front foot, there is every likelihood that he would have hit them.

Quartering 3

Quartering 4

Quartering 5

A nice straightforward quartering pair which have been thrown from the left side of the skeet house. These targets have been given a bit of air and as a consequence will nicely reach the peak of an arc together. They will virtually hang at this peak for a second before falling. Take them (back left-hand target first) as they reach the top of their rise.

TEAL

Here is a nice orthodox teal bird, rising straight in front of the shooter from a trap positioned beneath him. This particular gun seems to have everything right. His weight is slightly forward, he has measured the bird out at a nice height (remember, don't shoot a teal too quickly) and he will shortly take the bird as it approaches the top of its climb.

If this bird was followed by another on report, resist the impulse to rush it. For example, this teal could have coupled with a right to left crosser which would be released as soon as you have shot the teal. Your mind might start racing into thinking that you must make sure you shoot the teal in good time so that you can properly get at the crosser. In the cold light of day you might think that this is overstating the obvious, but I can assure you that I have seen it happen countless times. Just tell yourself to forget about that second target until you have shot the first.

Before you start shooting your sequence of targets, however, make sure that your stance is correct for both and, if it is necessary, for you to move your feet after the first shot. Then rehearse the movements so that you know exactly where and how you will take both targets. First concentrate only on the teal: break it and forget it. The only one that counts now is the crosser. Always take it one at a time.

Quartering 5

Teal

Crossing Pair

CROSSING PAIR

A crossing pair is a stand that will always produce a whole heap of scorecards that read 'Kill, Lost'! The main reason for this is confused thinking. The first shot is taken, often properly, and the second is very often a squeeze and a prayer.

Two in the air at once will always cause a degree of panic, but keep your cool – there is always more time than you think. I am not suggesting that you be a slow and deliberate shot, merely that you give yourself enough room to do the job properly. The chances are that you will shoot the first target according to the method and do everything prop-

erly. But what about the second? Watch a few others and you will see what happens – the gun simply leaps onto target number two, the cartridge is fired, the barrels stop, and the clay flies on unscathed.

So remember, after that first shot at the back bird your barrels, by virtue of your swinging momentum, will go straight onto the front bird. Don't shoot right away, give yourself just a little time to pick up its line, and then swing through and shoot. You'll be surprised how easy it can be!

The gun in the photograph seems to have the position about right, but I would advise a stance that is a little squarer to the targets. He might find himself straining slightly for the second bird.

11 English Skeet

English skeet is a super discipline in many ways. It sustains a large following but there are few who become its total master. Some deride it as straightforward and unchallenging, but while you know that each and every target takes a predetermined line of flight you can never be sure of hitting all twenty-five of every round. On the other hand, it offers the newcomer the opportunity of coming to terms with a variety of targets of which he can soon regularly break a good percentage. Hard work, patience, practice and concentration will see a steady climb in your scores until reaching the point where you are hitting in the twenty-three to twenty-five region every time out. But even then it can suddenly surprise you if you become over-confident and start to take it for granted.

Another nice thing about skeet is that you can shoot it with the same gun as all your sporting targets. Nine shot cartridges must be used throughout – but this is in the interests of fairness, not handicap. Nine is, in fact, the ideal size, as all targets will be killed at around twenty yards.

As a combination of singles and doubles from both right and left, skeet is also good practice for your sporting shooting. Don't fall into the trap of shooting targets in a particular way that might vary from your stance at sporting. You will see some people attempt all sorts of contortions, possibly because they once had an exceptionally good round of shooting that way. You can also shoot gun-up, i.e. call the bird with the gun already mounted. But I would strongly advise against this, as it will do your style a lot of damage.

METHOD

Because of the variety within the confines of the semi-circular round of twenty-five targets, gun fit and gun mounting will be of paramount importance. You will need to mount quickly but smoothly in the same spot each and every time. Don't do anything particularly special – simply remember to face the point at which you intend breaking the clay, and track each target before swinging through and killing it in the manner described earlier.

You can put yourself at an advantage for skeet by holding the gun at a predetermined point of its flight when calling for the target. This varies from stand to stand, but by and large it is a straight translation of common sense.

Concentration is a major factor in skeet. You really have to think about what you are doing – and think positively. Taking the gun too far back to the trap house on certain stands will cost you dearly – you will have to race to catch up with the target, as a result of which it is almost inevitable that you will flash and miss.

Remember that with skeet on every occasion you always see the target's first few yards of flight, which are also its fastest. For the purposes of actually shooting, forget those first few yards – and also forget the last. On certain stands, such as Station One high house, you will have ample opportunity of taking the target as it flies out in front of you. But the longer you leave it, the greater the margin for error. The cartridge pattern will start to break up, the target will lose speed and direction, and it also becomes more

STATION ONE

Your first bird is the high house – hold the gun up, look in the air.

Pick up its line, move through and shoot.

susceptible to the vagaries of the weather conditions. Take it while it is still on a positive line of flight, i.e. within twenty yards.

STEP BY STEP

Station One

Two singles, followed by a double. Always remember that for English skeet you only load one cartridge for a single, shoot the target then load another shell for the next single.

For the first single from the high house, you will stand so that your gun muzzles point towards the centre peg. This applies to the aproach work on all seven stations. Bring the muzzles back so that they are elevated to a

The low house bird is quite straightforward – take it at a nice easy shooting point.

point midway between the high house and the centre peg. Lift your head back so that your eyes are looking into the air immediately above you. You are then ready to call the first target. As the bird appears, follow it with your eyes, mounting so that it falls in line with your muzzles, then track, swing and shoot. Keep it smooth and neither rush the shot, nor make any attempt to ensure a kill by leaving it too late. The further away it travels the harder it will prove to kill. Have the confidence to shoot when it is right.

For the second single, which comes from the low house in the shape of a low angled driven target, take your muzzles so that they point in the direction of a quarter of the way in from the low house towards the centre. As the target appears, simply lift the gun into your shoulder tracking the target, swing through and shoot at a point when it has travelled just over half-way.

If you take the targets in this way, you will find that you are called upon to take two identical shots for the double. You should ideally kill them both in the same place as when you took them as singles.

If when shooting as singles you either shot too quickly or took too long, you will find that you have no sort of rhythm on the double.

Station Two

Two singles and a double. The procedure is virtually identical to the first station, only this time there will be no need to crane your head back for the high house. Don't look at the house itself – look at the point at which you expect the target to fly before it reaches your gun. If you look at the trap house you will be focusing on a stationary object which will ultimately have no bearing on your shooting other than to make it more difficult.

Again, hold your gun at a point midway between the high house and centre peg for the first single, and a quarter of the way out from the low house for the second single. A straightforward repeat of the two shots will take care of the double.

Station Three

Two singles. Your gun will need to be two-thirds of the way back from the centre peg towards the high house for the first target. You are now much squarer to the bird, and it becomes less of a quartering shot and more of a crosser. Don't forget to stand facing the centre peg, before pulling your muzzles back to the point ready for calling. For the low house, again hold the gun a quarter of the way out from the building to the centre peg.

Station Four

Two singles, followed by two doubles. Many people talk themselves out of this shot, but if you follow the rules of stance and mounting you will find that you will get a very satisfying full house. Take each target at a time, and this particularly applies to the double.

For the high house hold the muzzles of the gun at a point two-thirds of the way back to the high house, and again the holding position is a quarter of the way in from the low house. Don't think about a definite amount of lead. Targets can be slower at some grounds than others, and wind variations can also have a great effect on them. A right to left gale could mean that the high house bird struggles across the width of the layout, dropping badly at the end of the flight, while the low house bird whips up out of the trap almost like a springing teal. Hopefully, conditions will be much better than that; though this sort of sporting skeet can be a lot of fun – providing there is nothing serious at stake, like a championship title!

Basically the point I am making is that you should treat each target on its own merits. Look to your gun fit, stance and mounting to do the work for you, and the targets will almost break themselves. Be positive! On the double forget about the second target; concentrate on killing the first, then drop onto the other one. Some people shooting Station Four miss the high house bird of the double almost wholly as a result of lack of gun swing. As soon as the trigger is squeezed, the gun is stopped to move onto the low house bird. So remember – keep it moving.

Incidentally, I would prefer to take the high house target first, though if the wind conditions caused the low house bird to travel very fast I would opt for that one instead. In any event you will be required by the refereee to nominate which bird you intend to take first.

Station Five

Two singles. The high house is now your incoming target. After pointing your gun towards the centre peg, move the muzzles back to a point a quarter of the way in from the high house building. For the low house you will not need to be so close – two-thirds will be fine.

Station Six

Two singles, followed by two doubles. This time take your muzzles to a point a quarter of the way from the high house towards the centre, and half-way from the centre for the low house.

Keep concentrating on each and every bird, but don't be over-deliberate and re-member to stay smooth with your swing and tracking.

Station Seven

Two singles, followed by a double. You are now on the last station and getting close to the magical twenty-five. The targets are relatively easy after the more demanding centre stages, but don't relax – they still have to be broken.

For the high house move the muzzles back to a point a quarter of the way in, and for the low house simply hold them in the air above the centre peg about one and a half yards to its right. This latter instruction may seem a little odd, so let me explain. The high house target is pretty orthodox and you will shoot it at a point just over half-way. The low house bird, however, appears from near your shoulder and as it seems to travel in a straight line away from you the temptation and instinct is to poke at it. By holding your gun a little out of its line, you will be required to move the barrels and are consequently far less likely to miss the target.

If you have hit them all, some quick elementary mathematics will reveal that your tally is 24ex24. You are therefore given the option by the referee to take either of the Station Seven singles to make up the complete round of twenty-five. I'll give you no advice on that one. Choose whichever you prefer, but keep your cool and follow the simple procedure of positioning yourself correctly, holding the muzzles to the centre peg, moving to the given spot ready for calling the target, tracking it, swinging through and shooting. When you have hit your first twenty-five you will feel a very happy man indeed, and you will be eager to get another.

STATION TWO

The high bird target on Station Two is one of the easiest to miss.
Before calling, aim your gun at the centre peg.

Now take the gun back to point in a direction approximately midway
between the high house and centre peg, looking slightly further back to
the area in which you will see the target.

Mount the gun onto the back of the target.

Track it and shoot. By not taking your gun too far back you will have
avoided the common mistake of racing through and flashing in front.

STATION THREE

Similar procedure. Start at centre peg.

Move the gun back two-thirds of the way towards the high house, as this is more of a crossing target.

Mount and track.

Swing through and shoot, keeping that movement smooth and fluid.

The low house now needs a little more respect. Start with the gun a quarter of the way out from the trap house.

Mount and track nice and early.

Kill the target over the centre peg – and keep those barrels moving.

STATION FOUR

Not as hard as many believe – too many talk themselves out of it. Don't take your gun right back to the trap house.

Mount and track the target.

Move through and kill it over the centre – and remember to keep the gun moving, particularly when you have the double.

Get well into the target.

Pick it up and sit on it.

Swing through nicely and take it. Remember to be sharp but fluid for the double.

STATION FIVE

You are now reversing the process of the first three stands.

Having started with your gun a quarter of the way in, you can move onto the target nicely.

Take the target over the centre peg.

You needn't go back so far for the low house.

You will be shooting the bird in the region of the centre of the layout.

STATION SIX

This is another one where it is easy to slip. It is a quartering target and probably better for right-handers. To make sure, hold your gun towards the centre peg.

Don't take it back too far to the trap house.

Get onto it and move behind it.

Track and kill over the middle. Keep those barrels moving but don't flash
and don't poke. The incomer is straightforward, but don't leave it too late –
the flight can deviate badly in windy conditions.

STATION SEVEN

The point to remember here is to hold your gun slightly outside of the line of flight of the low house bird.

You can then swing onto it and take it nicely, rather than poke and miss. The high house incomer is a very straightforward clay, though again it should not be left too late in an effort to make sure of it.

SOME PROBLEMS WITH SKEET

If it was all as straightforward as I might seem to be suggesting, we would all be shooting twenty-five straight every time. Some do, but the majority don't – why is it? Many who don't do as well as they should are simply doing it wrongly. But there are other factors that can come into it.

Slow pulls and no birds

Slow pulls and no birds are the bane of the skeet shooter. When you are ready to call that target, you really are ready – like a rattlesnake coiled ready to strike; there is little that will stop you putting the gun in the shoulder and squeezing the trigger as the target reaches the allotted place. If it is a no bird and you shoot,

then according to the rules you have accepted it whether you hit it or not. Even the very best have come unstuck on this one – rightly or wrongly, this is the rule and rules are made to be adhered to. So be on the alert – remember to concentrate at all times. Likewise, if it was a slow pull, it may not have been spotted by the referee, and if you shoot it will be no good complaining afterwards. Check yourself and point it out to the official.

On the subject of officials, whatever you do don't get involved in a row with one. Think it out rationally before you start getting angry – he has made his decision and if reasoned and polite comment will not persuade him, then nothing will. If you end up having a blazing row, you will ruin your day's sport, and probably spoil the day for others into the bargain. If it is a major competition and you genuinely believe that

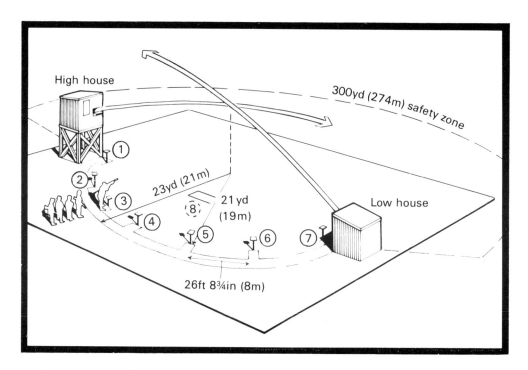

A typical skeet layout. Station 8 is used only in ISU skeet.

110

an error of judgement has been made then you have recourse to a jury. But be absolutely sure of yourself. It is all too easy to believe what you want to believe in a situation where a lot depends on one target.

Concentration

All of these problems will do much to upset your concentration. If you attempt to shoot when you are not mentally prepared there will be only one conclusion – lost targets. Similarly, while you will be on a squad of five shooters all enjoying themselves, when it comes to standing on the station and calling targets forget about everything other than killing that target. You have to be single-minded. If it is a big competition, it may be that the other four will be lost in their concentration. You should follow their example and not confuse commitment with anti-social behaviour. You can chat afterwards.

You might know someone who laughs and jokes his way through a round of practice and still scores twenty-four or twenty-five. But competition is very different and the tensions that tend not to show themselves in practice

Competition action – note how the squad members are keeping to themselves in order to concentrate solely on their shooting.

suddenly loom large. You will need your wits about you to stay calm and collected.

Always make sure that you have your gun and cartridges ready for when you are likely to be called upon to shoot; and take four or five spares with you in case you get some no birds.

Positive thinking plays an important role in all aspects of your shooting. Missing your first target is not the end of the world – you can still finish with a twenty-four. So when you miss a bird put it right out of your head and start thinking solely about hitting the next one.

You might receive advice or instruction during the the round. It will be well meant so appear appreciative, but if you are confident in the way you have been shooting, then stick to the method you know and make sure you are doing it to the best of your ability.

Practice targets

In a competition you will be given the option of taking two practice targets. I would recommend that you try for Station One high house, so that when you start you can do so in a confident manner.

Is Station Four really the hardest stand? The simple answer to that is 'No'. If you check on a number of scores at any given shoot you will find that the two most difficult stands are Two high and Six low. Both are awkward quartering targets and are often missed as a result of the shooter taking the muzzles too far back to the trap house. Consequently he will race after it when it rockets out of the trap house and almost certainly miss it in front. If you give the target a chance to get clear of the house before you mount and track it, you will find that relatively little lead is necessary.

12 Down-the-Line

Down-the-Line was the first recognised shooting discipline in this country, representing a simple evolutionary step forward from live pigeon trap shooting. Using an oscillating trap positioned sixteen yards in front of a line, the targets are thrown out in an arc of twenty-two degrees either side of an imaginary line directly in front of the trap. They travel to a range of between fifty and fifty-five yards. This means that their speed of flight will be in the region of fifty-five to sixty miles per hour. For many years DTL was the most popular form of clay pigeon shooting in this country and it still commands a very large following. I very much enjoy a round of trap and DTL can teach you many things.

DTL is an ideal discipline for a novice in that good scores are possible quite early on, and it will teach the novice exactly how his gun mounting and sight pictures are related to the killing of a target. He will also learn the importance of concentration, for in DTL you have twenty-five targets at a time (not ten as in sporting) and you will be standing on a line for about twenty minutes. No one will be talking during the shooting and if you start to put a good sequence of first barrel kills together, one of two things can happen: you either become over-confident or you suddenly discover that you are not as calm and self-assured as you thought you were. It is the application of concentration and overcoming the sheer inward pressure that gives such enormous satisfaction to anyone hitting twenty-five first barrel kills. Practice shooting is one thing, but shooting in a competition is a very different matter.

Unlike a sporting competition, you will have seen and broken all the targets before – so you know you can do it. But actually getting a 25/75 in a competitive situation is quite an achievement. (The scoring is three points for a first barrel kill and two points for a second barrel.)

YOUR GUN

While many club shooters will have a go at DTL with their usual sporting gun (particularly with the advent of multi-choke guns), if

Russ Martin, one of England's best shots in competitive action on a DTL layout. Note the easy stance, but still in total command of the gun.

you hope to achieve any sort of success at the sport then you should invest in a trap gun. The essential difference from your sporting gun is that it will be a larger weapon overall. It will have barrels of 30 inches (some even prefer 32 inches), a meatier stock, a weight of around 8lb, and it is built to shoot slightly high.

The advantage of having a heavier gun will soon become apparent once you start shooting trap targets. A lighter weapon would whip through the clays and you would probably shoot over the top – most misses are, in fact, over the top in this discipline. A

DTL target races out of the trap house, rises and then flattens out. Many, on their first attempts at the sport, rush after the clay and race right through it. When they shoot, the clay is actually either level or falling. The longer barrels of 30 inches are a great aid in their facility to point out a target, and they will also keep your style smoother. The overall size of the gun will also help to absorb the recoil that after twenty targets could otherwise start to have a significant effect on second barrel kills, and will spare your shoulder if you are using 'thumpy' trap cartridges.

People tend to develop their own style of shooting DTL. Pictured here is Keith Bond, a fabulous shooter of this discipline who in 1985 achieved the rare distinction of winning both the English and British titles. You will note that Keith adopts an exaggerated style whereby his right arm is upwards of a right angle to his body. It works superbly for him, but don't attempt to imitate him – just because it does the trick for Keith there is no reason to assume that it will turn you into a winner. Only time and practice will offer that kind of answer. Do the basics properly then after a while you can make the final adjustments.

Choke

Your chokings should be ¾ and full (though you can get away with more open chokes). You want a nice tight pattern for the retreating target, so that if a second barrel is necessary you have still enough action where it counts to break the clay.

Cartridges

Choose a well-known make seven or seven and a half shot. If you have been doing sporting shooting then I would advise that you stick to whatever trap load has proved your favourite choice. You will know its capabilities and that will obviously be a help.

It might be stating the obvious, but make sure that you have enough cartridges with you when you are called to shoot. Take two boxes – they won't spoil if you don't use them all.

There is no real need to invest in any of the extra special super loads that are available on the market. They will cost you a lot of money and they are of no significant advantage for DTL. These cartridges are the choice of the Olympic trap experts, who need something up their sleeve for this extremely demanding discipline. Though on a personal note, I am of the belief that a good standard trap load of one of the better makes is usually adequate. It is the confidence instilled by having the best that proves the biggest asset.

SHOOTING THE TARGETS

Your trap gun will shoot slightly high so that you can keep sight of the retreating rising target when you actually pull the trigger. It is purpose-built for this specific job.

There is little doubt that for any form of trap there is a distinct advantage to be gained from being able to practise at fixed targets. This is generally not possible in a club situation – and certainly not on a competition day. Ideally, if you can practise on a fixed target, by taking it a peg at a time you can tackle and master all the different angles so that on seeing them in a proper round you will know how to respond. Starting on peg three with a fixed target going directly away, you can first learn to master the art of shooting the trap target. As with all shooting it is again the same three ingredients that will dictate your degree of proficiency – gun fit, mounting and stance.

Stance

One of the biggest problems in trap shooting is that of people holding their gun in position, then dropping their cheek onto the stock. This canting of the eyes can only mean one thing – missed targets. You don't see people walking round with their head tilted to one side, so how on earth can they be expected to shoot clay pigeons doing the same thing? Unfortunately, until it is pointed out no one actually realises that they are doing it.

Adopt a nice relaxed stance, with your weight on the front foot (left foot for right-handers) and your gun will come into your cheek and shoulder. Stand comfortably, looking down the rib and seeing just enough of it so that you can see the clay sit nicely on the end when it is in flight. The position of your stance will be such that the top half of your body can pivot and enable you to swing onto those angled birds without any undue strain or awkwardness.

As with skeet, you will find that people adopt all sorts of idiosyncratic positions, probably because they happened to shoot well one day when they tried doing something different. For goodness' sake don't make any attempt to emulate anyone who favours an unorthodox stance. He may appear to be shooting quite well, but by copying, you could be making it difficult for yourself. Remember, at all times, to endeavour to keep it simple.

Once you have mastered the straight target from peg three, you should attempt fixed straight targets from the other pegs. Then try a right-hand target from peg one (in effect a straight target) and, keeping the angle of the clay the same, move round the pegs until you get to peg five. Switch the trap to throw a left-hander, and reverse the sequence, i.e. peg five to peg one. You will now have covered virtually every angle and know (or have a good idea) of how to react to all of them.

Remember to keep a nice upright stance, weight leaning onto the front foot. You will be holding your gun in positions on an imaginary arc above the trap house for each target (as shown on page 120). From peg one you hold it above the corner, peg two half-way to the middle, peg three over the middle (but not too high), peg four half-way from the middle to the right, and peg five above the right corner. This is simply to give you an advantage. If you hold it above the left corner, for example, you just lift for a right-hander, and if it is a left-hander you have reduced the necessary amount of gun movement to a minimum. This will prove a real advantage on peg five. For a right-handed shot the right-hand target from peg five is without doubt the most awkward.

Here, I am awaiting my turn to shoot. Some people prefer not to look at the clays as they wait – they feel it may affect their shot inasmuch as subconsciously suggesting a predetermined direction of the target, i.e. the last one was straight, so the next will be a right-hander. There is no sequence so you can put that out of your head. If you can ignore the other people shooting I feel that it is not a bad idea to closely observe the general flight of the targets as you wait.

My turn and I hold the gun as if to mount for a sporting target. I will then slide the gun into my shoulder.

The gun is now firmly in position. Note that I am on peg five so the line of my barrels is pointing in the direction of an area immediately above the right-hand corner of the trap house. This means that whatever target I receive my barrel movement will have been reduced to a minimum.

It is as well that I held the barrel at this point as the target was a right-hander and consequently a big swing of the gun was not necessary. Remember to keep your barrels moving for this target.

This photograph illustrates the point that if you have positioned yourself correctly then you will have made the actual shooting of the target a much easier process. I am positioned on peg two and as the bird on this occasion is a slight right hander I merely lift the barrels into it and pull the trigger.

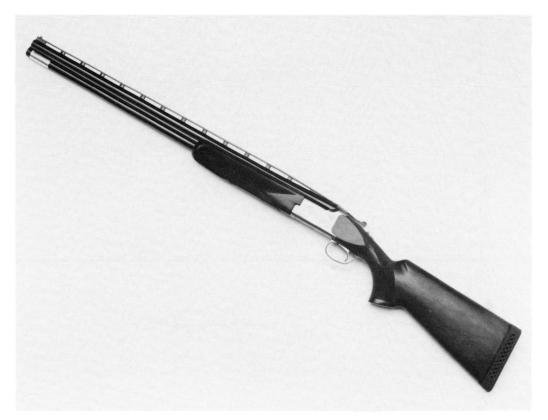

The gun I used for this sequence is a Browning Citori with a high rib. This type of rib is very popular in America and I expect that it will become increasingly so in this country. While the gun may look quite different to a conventionally ribbed model, in fact it shoots little differently. What it does offer, however, is an excellent plane of vision. Because you know that all of the targets are rising and going away there is no real need to take the barrels into account when taking your shot. With a raised rib you are completely unaware of the barrels that are carrying it. A consequence of this is that it is quicker to read a target and get onto it. Remember though, that Keith Bond, arguably our most successful and best DTL shot, uses only his conventional flat ribbed Beretta. They make a formidable combination. So choose the gun that suits you best.

It is fact of nature that a right-hander has a tendency to favour right to left birds, while a left-hander is better at left to right targets. If you think about it, this is simply because these are more natural movements in both cases. Also, if you were to take a right-handed shot swinging onto a left to right crosser from a fixed position, he could easily lift the stock of the gun off his face. Moving the other way it will stick closely to his cheek. This is why some American coaches will even go so far as suggesting that on peg four, right-handers should hold their gun over a point maybe three-quarters of the way from the centre of the trap house to its right edge. While from peg five they should even hold the gun up to a foot outside of the right-hand corner. Personally I feel that this is overdoing it, but you can see the point I am making. To keep gun movement to a minimum you need all the advantages you can get.

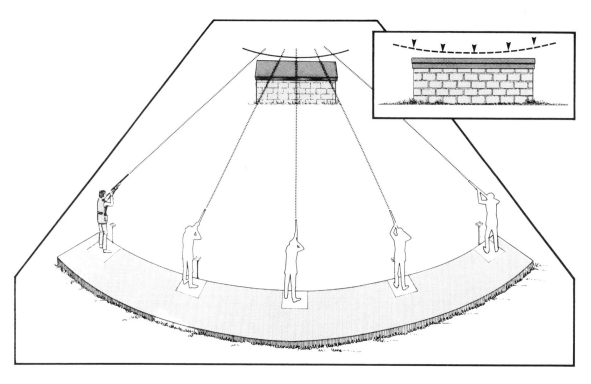

This illustration shows the kind of shooting position which should be taken
at each peg. Note the position of the feet in each instance and also the
point of aim of the gun when calling for the target.

SOME PROBLEMS
WITH TRAP

These can be numerous. When you get out
on a line of shooters and things start to go
wrong, it can be a very lonely place. Panic
appears from nowhere. You will have arrived
at the ground with all the confidence in the
world. You hit your first two or three targets,
then for no apparent reason you miss a bird,
you then get a scratchy kill, a clean kill, a
second barrel, another scratchy one and it all
starts to fall apart. The tendency is often to
alter your style in an effort to improve. You
notice that the gun at the next peg is shooting
quickly and grinding the targets to dust. So
you think that you have been shooting too
slowly, and consequently you speed up. This

might have the desired immediate effect but
as you are not accustomed to shooting in that
way it will soon start to fade. You lose
confidence in your cartridges when you see
the clay breaking into two or three big bits
instead of a cloud of smoke.

Generally, you lose all confidence and
when you call your next target your mind is
all over the place. You are thinking about all
the things that are going wrong and you
simply want to call a halt to it and start all
over again. This is clearly impossible, so stop
and think. You know how well you normally
shoot, and you have an established gun and
cartridge combination. The targets might
vary a little from ground to ground, but it is
usually the backdrop which may appear to
make them look more different than they
actually are.

Mental check

So what are you doing wrong? Make a mental check back on all the important factors – your gun fit is correct (once established this ceases to be a variable) but what about your stance and mounting. Are you standing correctly? Are you canting your head? Are you lifting your head when you shoot? The latter is a very common problem when the confidence starts to slip, and it is a particularly common cause of missed second barrel shots. Always keep that head tight to the stock so that if you fail to connect with the clay first time, you are still in the correct position for the second barrel kill.

Have your muzzles started to drop? When your mind is full of all sorts of things (particularly despondency) you may find that you are holding your muzzles on the roof of the trap house. Consequently you will be racing after your targets. So snap out of it. Go through your mental check list, and get back into your usual rhythm as soon as possible.

Rhythm

Another problem area in shooting with a squad is that your rhythm can get upset in another way. You might have a trouble-maker on your line – usually someone who cannot accept that he is shooting below par: it is always someone else's fault. This is a

After the squad has completed their 25 targets, all guns will go to check their total with the scorer. Apart from personal curiosity this is always advisable. Don't take it for granted that the scorer will share your opinion as to how many you hit (or second barrelled). If there is any discrepancy it should be raised immediately. You might on the other hand be in for a pleasant surprise and find that you have scored more than you thought!

Taking a shot from the centre peg. This chap has got it absolutely right and he will probably smoke the target. This is another satisfying aspect of DTL – it is the only discipline where time after time you know exactly where you are breaking the target; and it is a good feeling when you are grinding them to dust!

particular problem with trap as you are dependent to a degree on the other four guns. If all goes smoothly you will find that you can slot into a nice groove.

You will often find that top shots prefer to shoot together. They establish a nice even pattern, so that they know when it is their turn to shoot without even thinking about it. Also, the shooting of targets efficiently in a regular sequence is infectious. You become confident. Conversely, if you are on a line with a trouble-maker and a couple of shots who are struggling, then locking yourself away to form any sort of pattern becomes a little more difficult. But in such circumstances don't make excuses to yourself – the targets are there to be hit, and if you don't give your best you will be letting yourself

down. A good lesson to learn from this is to try and get into a good squad.

Keep on your toes too for slow pulls. If the button pusher is not doing his job properly there is nothing wrong in refusing to shoot the target. If you get a very slow pull there is a good chance that you will miss it – particularly if you have established a rhythm. Point it out nicely and you will be given the bird again. Likewise, if a clay is ground to bits as it leaves the trap, take a deep breath, give yourself time and check your routine once again before calling 'Pull'.

Think clearly and confidently, don't be rushed or harassed – just keep it simple and you will find that things might go rather well for you.

Appendix: CPSA Rules

As I mentioned earlier, anyone taking up clay pigeon shooting is well recommended to join the Clay Pigeon Shooting Association. Any sport is as good as its governing body, and clay pigeon shooting needs the CPSA more nowadays than probably ever before. Because of the numbers now involved we can no longer afford to take what in many cases has been an amateurish approach to clay pigeon shooting. It needs to become much more sophisticated or professional (in the nicest sense of the word). In order for this to happen the CPSA needs the full support of all who shoot clay targets.

The CPSA runs all of the sport's major competitions, decides the way in which our disciplines are to be run and publishes the rules which, with their kind permission, I have included as the final section of the book. (These rules are correct at the time of writing, but are subject to alteration by the CPSA.) Not only do they offer useful reference, I am sure you will find that they make interesting reading in their own right. Whether the shoots which you attend are registered or informal, you would be well-advised to always think in terms of shooting according to the rules. Far from being inhibiting, you will find it a pleasure to be shooting properly. They are the etiquette of good clay pigeon shooting.

ENGLISH SPORTING

1   **Targets**. FITASC targets (mini, midi, battue, rocket and rabbit targets) may be used as well as normal ISU targets for skeet and Olympic trap. The FITASC targets shall not exceed thirty per cent of the total number of targets in the competition.

2   **Targets Thrown**. Targets may be thrown as singles, report pairs, following pairs or as simultaneous pairs. Targets will be thrown by silent and non-visible instruction by the referee after the shooter has pronounced the word 'ready'. The release shall take place at any time up to three seconds after the shooter has pronounced the word 'ready'.

3   **Guns**. All shotguns including automatics are allowed providing their calibre does not exceed 12 gauge. No handicap will be given to shooters using guns of less than 12 gauge. Automatic guns must not be loaded with more than two cartridges. Straps on guns are forbidden except for handicapped persons who have been given express permission by the organisers. In the case of a shooter not complying with these regulations all targets on that particular stand or stands shall be counted as lost. It is forbidden to use another person's gun without his permission.

4   **Cartridges**. The load of cartridges shall not exceed 32 grammes of shot. The shot shall be spherical shot of normal production lead, diameter between 2 and 2.6mm, English sizes 6-9: plated shot may be used. Home loads may not be used. The referee may at any time take an unfired cartridge out of a shooter's gun for examination. If the cartridge is found not to comply with the regulations, all targets on that particular stand will be counted as lost.

5   **A Report Pair**. A pair where the second target is launched at the sound of the gun firing at the first target.

6   **A Following Pair**. A pair where the second target is launched as soon and as safely as possible after the first target, from the same trap.

7   **A Simultaneous Pair**. A pair where both targets are launched simultaneously.

8 **Trajectories**. At each stand, the trajectories shall be the same for each shooter in height, distance and speed. It must be possible for all the targets to be hit within the effective range of a 12-bore shotgun. Before a shoot, organisers will establish a scheme for the trajectories of targets: these trajectories, established and calculated in calm weather, may be altered by wind, but if so altered, will remain regular targets.

9 **Target Killed**. The target is killed when it has been launched and the shooter has shot it according to the rules, and at least one visible bit of it has broken off, or it has been totally or partially pulverised.

10 **Target Missed**
(a) When it has not been hit.
(b) If only dusted or deflected.
(c) If the shooter is unable to fire because he has left the safety catch on, has forgotten to load or cock, if the gun has been insufficiently broken or closed or if the shooter has forgotten to take the necessary measures to load the chamber (when he uses a single barrel gun).
(d) If it is the fourth or more malfunction of the gun or ammunition occurring at the same stand.
(e) If the shooter is unable to fire his second shot, having not put in a second cartridge, or if he has not cancelled the locking device of the loading chamber of an automatic weapon, or if the safety catch engages due to recoil of the first shot, or if the second cartridge is ejected by the recoil or opened and emptied by the recoil for any other reason.
(f) If the second shot cannot be fired because a shooter using a single trigger gun has not released the trigger sufficiently having fired his first shot.
(g) If the shooter in the case of a malfunction, opens it himself or touches the safety catch before the referee has examined the gun.
(h) If the shot is fired for another reason which does not give right to another target.
(i) If the shooter (without legitimate reason) does not shoot at a regular double.

(j) If the shooter (without legitimate reason) does not shoot the second target of a regular double, the result of the first is scored, and the second declared lost.

11 **Shooting Position.** The shooter will position himself within the area of the shooting stand. He is allowed to load his gun only on the stand, his gun always pointing down the range, and only when the referee has given the signal to start shooting. In no case may a shooter move to the stand before the preceding shooter has left the stand and it is his turn to shoot. Shooting stands shall be clearly defined squares of 0.91 m side.

12 **Gun Position.** Gun position in relation to the shoulder shall be optional when the shooter calls for the target, providing it complies with rule 11 (shooting position).

13 **Viewing Point.** Any shooter who has had an opportunity to see targets on any stand, i.e. at the commencement of the competition each day, shall have the right to be shown it/them. He must watch these from a position specified by the shoot organiser.

14 **Shooting and Sighting.** Shooting and sighting practice is not allowed. A shooter can only fire on his turn, and only when a target has been launched. It is forbidden to aim or shoot other shooters' targets; it is also forbidden to aim or fire on purpose at living animals/birds. Any such action shall lead to immediate disqualification without the return of entry fee.

15 **Roll Call.** On roll call, the shooter must be ready to fire immediately and must take with him sufficient ammunition and equipment for the stand. The referee shall warn the following shooter to be prepared to shoot.

16 **Gun Malfunctions.** The shooter shall be allowed three gun or ammunition malfunctions not attributable to him on each stand without being penalised. The fourth or later

malfunction shall be counted as lost or pair lost.

In the case of jamming of the gun which on the referee's decision cannot be repaired on the spot without being the shooter's fault, the shooter will be allowed to fire with another gun if he can get one immediately. Otherwise he may shoot his remaining targets later but only with the referee's permission.

In the case of misfiring or malfunctioning, the shooter has to remain where he is, the gun pointed down the range, not opened, and without touching the safety catch before the referee has examined the gun.

Two cartridges can be used on each single target, but the shooter will only be allowed two cartridges for each double.

In the case of a gun or ammunition malfunction on a single target, provided the shooter has been able to fire one shot, the result shall be scored.

In doubles the shooter has the right to shoot either of the targets first. Should the shooter kill both targets together with either the first or second shot, then the result will be scored pair killed.

In a double, the shooter having missed his first target may fire his second cartridge at the same target.

When shooting a report pair or following pair, the shooter will have the right if he misses the first target to fire his second cartridge at the same target, the result being scored on the first target, the second target being counted as lost.

17 **No Target.** The clay will be 'No Target' and a new target will be launched, the shooter having fired or not if:

(a) the target is broken at the start

(b) the target is launched from the wrong trap

(c) two targets are launched simultaneously when a single should have been thrown

(d) the target is definitely of another colour than the targets used for the competition at that stand

(e) the first or second target of a double is irregular

(f) two targets are launched simultaneously during a report pair or a following pair

(g) the target is launched before the shooter has said 'ready'

(h) the target is launched after a delay of more than three seconds

(i) the target zigzags, or its initial speed is not sufficient, or if its trajectory is irregular

(j) the shooter misses his first target and this target collides with the second before the shooter has fired his second shot.

In the case of a 'No Target' in any form of doubles the shooter will be asked to fire a second double to determine the scores of the two shots. This will also apply in the case of malfunction of gun or ammunition not attributable to the shooter, provided that it is not the fourth time on that stand.

The referee may also order the launching of a new target when:

(a) the shooter has been materially disturbed

(b) another shooter fires at the same target

(c) the referee cannot decide for any reason if the target has been killed or lost.

The referee cannot in any case give a 'No Target' if the shooter has missed for any reason other than the ones stated in the 'No Target' rules.

The shooter must not turn round before he has opened his gun and removed the cartridges. In the case of a 'No Target' the gun must be opened and the cartridges removed. It can be closed only when firing resumes.

18 **Referee's Duties.** The referee's decision can be brought up before the jury on paper. If the jury finds the protest valid it can give the referee directions for future decisions or elect a new referee or finally over-rule the referee's decision, insofar as this does not concern lost or killed targets or irregular targets, where the referee's decision is final.

If the shooter or the team's captain does not agree with the referee about a shot, a complaint must be made immediately the incident occurs, by raising the arm and saying 'protest'. The referee must then stop the shooting and give his decision. In no case will it be possible to pick up a target to see if it has been shot.

The referee under the control of the jury shall see to the application of the rules, keep the onlookers silent and out of the way, and see that the shooters have a clear view from the shooting stand.

If a shooter or team's captain is of the opinion that the score announced is not correct, he must immediately make a complaint to the referee. The referee must then immediately check the result after which he makes his decision known. If the complainant does not agree with this decision he has to present the jury with a short written notice.

A referee can, in exceptional circumstances, interrupt the shooting at any time. This interruption may only take place when a shooter has finished shooting and before another one commences.

The referee may be assisted by a marker, particularly in big championships. The principal function of the marker is to keep a record on a score sheet of the results of each shot as it is called by the referee.

The referee has to decide immediately if a new target is to be launched due to irregularity. He should say 'No Target' before the shooter fires.

19 **Jury**. At every competition a jury of five shooters representative of the shooters present shall be appointed. A Chairman shall be elected who shall have a casting vote in the case of equal voting. The jury can make valid decisions when the Chairman and two members are present. In urgent cases two members of the jury who arrive at a unanimous decision may take such a decision after consultation with the referee of the stand concerned.

Any protest to the jury shall be accompanied by a protest fee of £1 non-returnable if the protest is lost.

The duties of the jury are as follows:
(a) Verify that before shooting begins, the stands conform with the regulations and the arrangements in general are suitable and correct.

(b) See during shooting that rules are adhered to and that guns, ammunition and targets are examined by random test.
(c) Make decisions in connection with technical defects or other disturbances in the shooting if these are not resolved by the referee.
(d) Deal with protests.
(e) Make decisions regarding penalties if a shooter does not adhere to the rules or deports himself in an unsportsmanlike manner.
(f) To make sure that at least two members of the jury are always present on the shooting ground.

If the shooter uses guns or ammunition not corresponding to rules, all shots fired with these weapons or ammunition are considered 'lost'. If the jury finds that the violation has been done intentionally it can disqualify the shooter. If, however, the jury finds the shooter could not be aware of the violation and has not gained real advantage, it may be decided to accept the result under condition that the fault is corrected and acknowledged.

Other than in rules concerning disqualification, violation of the rules will normally incur first a warning from the referee or a member of the jury. In the case of further or more important offences, the jury may fine the shooter with a lost target or in more serious cases disqualify him from the competition.

If a shooter does not present himself after being called three times, he will normally forfeit three targets, taken from the first three killed targets of that stand. The jury may give him the opportunity to shoot his remaining targets later, at a time specified by the referee. If the jury notices a shooter deliberately delaying the competition or acting in a dishonest or dishonourable, or intemperate manner, it may give him a warning or fine him one target, or disqualify him from the competition.

When the jury fines the shooter one target and does not specify which one in particular, the first killed target after the verdict must be considered lost. If the shooter has finished the day's shooting, the target is deducted from the last stand on the card.

20 **Ties.** For first place will be decided by shooting as follows: a stand will be drawn out and the tied shooters will shoot the stand again. If this does not resolve the tie, then it will be shot again, miss and out. All other results for trophies or article prizes, will be by shoot off. All divisible prizes, by add and divide.

21 **Team Ties.** Shall be resolved as for individual ties, by shooting the tie between the highest scorers of each team as in the rule on ties.

All shooters are supposed to have acquainted themselves with the current regulations which apply to the shooting under English Sporting Rules.

By taking part in the competition, they accept the penalties and other consequences resulting from violation of the rules and referee's order. The rules shall be posted in a prominent position.

DOWN-THE-LINE

Historical

DTL, as it is called, first appeared in Gt Britain when the Inanimate Bird Shooting Association was formed in 1892. It proved extremely popular and was even shot under floodlights in the early 1930s at the White City Stadium. It is the longest running clay shooting international competition.

It is usually the type of clay shooting that new clubs first install and many newcomers to the sport of clay pigeon shooting first try.

Choosing and setting out a ground

The background for a Down-the-Line layout should be a major consideration. It is difficult to follow the flight of a target thrown in the direction of nearby trees or buildings and this should be remembered when choosing the site. A flat open field, with the trap set pointing north-

east to avoid sun-ray interference, provides the ideal setting for Down-the-Line shooting. A minimum 'danger zone' of 300 yards in front of each trap is necessary, based on the assumption that the regulation cartridge load will not be exceeded.

For a standard layout the five firing marks should be set in an arc of 16 yards radius from the trap, 3 yards apart, with the centre of No. 3 firing mark in a direct line between the trap and the firing stand.

When more than one layout is installed there should be at least 40 yards between each trap.

A combination of skeet and DTL facilities can be obtained in one layout by installing the DTL trap midway between the two skeet trap houses. This makes an ideal and neat setting when the two forms of shooting are to be incorporated.

The club house or marquee should be erected at a distance sufficient to prevent conversation disconcerting the competitors.

DTL procedure

With the trap and targets set as shown in 'Setting the trap' the shooters in the squad shoot in turn (down-the-line) at single targets (see Doubles) released, at permitted varying angles, on command.

1 **Shooting order.** The shooters comprising the squad shall stand at the designated firing marks from one to five (from left to right facing the trap) in the order in which their names appear on the score card. All guns shall be open and empty.

2 **Shooting DTL**
(a) When the referee is satisfied that all is ready and correct he shall call 'line ready'.
(b) All competitors may then load with two cartridges.
(c) The first competitor shall adopt his shooting stance (see Gun position) and call 'Pull!'
(d) Whereupon the puller (unless acoustic release is in use), who shall be behind the line of shooters, shall immediately release a target.
(e) The first shooter may shoot at this target

in flight with one or two shots. The resulting score is recorded.

If he scores a 'kill' with his first shot he shall be awarded three points. If he scores a 'kill' with his second shot he shall be awarded two points. If he fails to 'kill' the target with either shot, it shall be 'lost' and he shall be awarded zero points (see Scoring).

3 (a) Provided that a no bird has not been called and the referee has announced the result of the shot, the shooter on the second firing mark may then follow the same procedure, followed afterwards by the third shooter and repeated for Nos. 4 and 5.

(b) After No. 5 has shot, No. 1 shall call for a target and this sequence is followed by all the shooters in the squad until the required number of targets have been shot at.

(c) Each competitor shall shoot at each firing mark:
(i) In a 10 bird stage – 2 targets.
(ii) In a 15 bird stage – 3 targets.
(iii) In a 20 bird stage – 4 targets.
(iv) In a 25 bird stage – 5 targets.

4 At such point an audible signal shall be given and the referee shall call 'change!'

Each shooter (except No. 5) then moves to the firing mark next on his right and No. 5 takes the place of No. 1.

5 When leaving the firing marks each shooter *must* ensure that his gun is open.

The shooter leaving No. 5 firing mark to take up his position at No. 1 firing mark must move to that position by walking *behind the line of shooters with his gun open and empty of cartridges or cases*.

6 When the referee is satisfied that all is in order and *all* the shooters are again in proper position, he shall call 'line ready' and shall do so after each change and before the commencement of shooting.

7 The No. 1 of the squad (after the first move and standing at No. 2 firing mark) commences the second round, at the end of which

the squad again moves to the right. He also commences the third and remaining rounds and he finishes at No. 5 firing mark.

8 When all the members of the squad have shot at the required number of targets from each firing mark this will conclude the shooting of this particular stage. *At this point all guns must be opened and emptied of any cartridges or cases.*

9 The number of stages in a competition is as follows:
(a) For a 50 bird competition 2 stages of 25 targets.
(b) For a 75 bird competition 3 stages of 25 targets.
(c) For a 100 bird competition 4 stages of 25 targets.
And so on.

For competitions of less than 50 birds the organising committee may decide on the number of stages to be shot so long as the equity of the competition is maintained.

Ammunition

(a) Cartridge specification. Maximum bore 12 gauge. Maximum size of shot 2.6mm diameter (No. 6 English). Maximum load 32 grammes ($1\frac{1}{8}$ oz). The shot pellets may be plated.
(b) Home loaded, black powder, incendiary or tracer cartridges are not permitted at registered events or CPSA competitions and can be prohibited by the club or ground organising any other type of event if so desired.
(c) Not more than two cartridges may be placed in any part of a gun at any one time (see Penalties).
(d) The referee or jury may inspect the competitor's cartridges at any time, without giving a reason.

Balk

Any occurrence which in *the opinion of the referee* materially handicaps the competitor after he calls 'pull', if it deters him from shooting or distracts him at the moment of shooting.

(a) After any balk the referee shall declare a no bird.

(b) Misfires (under certain limitations as set forth in the Rules) are balks.

(c) Only the competitor directly concerned may claim a balk.

(d) Any claim must be made immediately after the incident in question. Later claims, however presented, will *not* be permitted.

(e) A claim for a balk which is upheld also constitutes a no bird and will entitle the competitor to a repeat target.

(f) A claim for a balk which is *not* upheld will be scored lost.

Competition

Wherever the word 'competition' is used in the following rules, it refers to a single event on a programme, to an entire one-day programme, or to the programme for any one tournament, and must always be so construed by those in charge of such 'competition'.

Competitor (*see* Penalties)

(a) It is a condition of entry that he shall observe the rules as herein described and any others that may apply especially for the event.

(b) He shall shoot and behave in a safe manner at all times.

(c) He may load only at the firing mark and when permitted by the referee.

(d) Each competitor is allowed only 15 seconds to call for his target after the result of the preceeding shooters target has been announced by the referee (or if he is No. 1 in the squad after the referee's call of 'line ready').

(e) He shall remove any cartridge case or unfired cartridge from his gun before turning from the firing point.

(f) He shall be at the firing mark within three minutes of being duly notified.

(g) He shall take sufficient cartridges with him to complete his round.

(h) He shall shoot only from his proper firing mark at the designated clay targets in flight.

(i) He shall not shoot at or 'sight' any birds, beasts, other objects, or other competitors' clay targets.

(j) He shall remain at his final firing mark until *all* the competitors in the squad have completed the stage.

Disqualification (*see* Penalties)

Disqualification entails the forfeiture of all entrance monies and rights in the competition to which it relates.

Duly notified

A competitor is 'duly notified' to compete when his name is called out by a referee, scorer or other person authorised to do so.

To assist notifying competitors it is strongly recommended that a visible squad marker board be used and kept up to date.

(a) If a 'squad hustler' is provided, it is a matter of courtesy only and does not relieve the competitor of responsibility. It is the duty of each competitor to be ready to compete promptly when called upon to do so (*see* Penalties).

(b) A competitor shall arrive at his proper firing mark and be ready to shoot within three minutes of being duly notified.

(c) If he is absent after this time his name shall be called out loudly twice in succession by the referee.

If the shooter is still not present 15 seconds after this he shall be declared 'absent' and the referee shall without further delay call 'line ready' and shooting shall then commence.

(d) (i) To participate in a stage, a competitor must be at his proper firing mark at the time the referee calls 'line ready'.

(ii) No competitor shall be permitted to shoot the stage if he arrives after this.

(iii) He may be permitted to shoot the missed stage at a later time to be determined by the ground organisation in consultation with the jury. (*see* Penalties).

Firing mark

(a) A clearly designated reasonably flat area measuring 3ft × 3ft (91cm × 91cm), the front centre of which is 16 yards (14.6m) from the centre of the pivot point of the trap when set to throw a straight away target.

(b) The area from which the competitor shall shoot. The competitor must have both feet entirely within this area when he calls for the target and until the completion of the shot (or shots) at that target (*see* Penalties – Foot Fault).

Guns

A smooth bore gun having a barrel not less than 24 inches in length not being an air gun.

(a) Shotguns used in competitions or events organised by the CPSA or clubs or grounds affiliated to the CPSA must conform to the pertinent Firearms Acts.

(b) Within these limitations all types of shotguns may be used provided the calibre does not exceed 12 bore.

(c) Barrels with attached ventilated recoil eliminators are prohibited.

(d) Automatic shotguns shall be so adjusted that their operation does not inconvenience other competitors.

(e) A shotgun that has malfunctioned twice in any stage of the competition should not be used unless it has been satisfactorily repaired. A competitor having a third or subsequent malfunction in any one stage must abide by the result.

(f) A properly functioning shotgun may not be exchanged for another in the course of a stage, unless the referee shall give his permission.

Gun position

The gun may be held in any safe position, but it is usual to adopt the 'gun-up' position, that is with the gun butt into the shoulder, loaded, safety catch off, the barrels pointed towards the target flight area and ready to call.

The jury

A jury of at least five competent persons shall be appointed prior to the commencement of any registered event.

(a) The jury should consist where possible of one member of the ground management, one referee, one member of the Executive Regional or County Committee where possible and the remainder of the jury of knowledgeable and competent shooters who are listed in the current CPSA averages.

(b) The jury is responsible for:
   (i) Setting target flights, angles and distances according to the current rules and prevailing conditions.
   (ii) Awarding penalties.
   (iii) Arbitrating on complaints or protests lodged.
   (iv) Deciding on the competence or otherwise of the *referees* and *scorers* and may remove or replace any of these at any time during the competition.
   (v) Deciding on the intended meaning of these rules when there is a requirement for interpretation.

(c) The jury may not overrule a referee as to whether a target is hit or not.

Killed target

A regular target that in the opinion of the referee has at least a visible piece broken from it, or is completely reduced to dust, or has a visible piece broken from it which is reduced to dust, by the competitors' shot.

(a) A target which has some dust removed from it by the shot but remains otherwise intact is not a killed target.

(b) Shot marks on a target in a 'pick-up' are not evidence of a killed target and will not be considered as such.

Lost target

A regular target that is not a killed target after having been fired upon in accordance with these rules.

A regular target shall be declared 'lost' when:
(a) The target remains unbroken after being fired at.
(b) The competitor fails to fire for any reason due to his own fault or negligence.
(c) The competitor after an apparent misfire opens his gun or moves the safety catch before

handing the gun to the referee.

(d) A competitor suffers a third or subsequent malfunction or misfire in the same stage.

Magazine gun

A single barrelled shotgun capable of holding more than one cartridge at any one time.

Malfunction (*see* Misfire)

Failure of a shotgun to fire the cartridge due to some defect of the *shotgun* mechanism.

(a) (i) An ammunition defect is not a malfunction.

   (ii) Any cause due to the shooter's fault is not a malfunction.

   (iii) 'Jarring back' – of the safety catch on the report of the first shot is *not* a malfunction.

(b) The shooter is allowed a total of two malfunctions (*or* misfires) in any one stage. Thereafter he must abide by the result.

(c) Second barrel malfunction. An allowable malfunction on the second shot shall be resolved by:

   (i) The target being declared a no bird.

   (ii) The competitor shall then repeat the target and the result of the second shot only shall be scored.

(d) General. Any shotgun which has a malfunction which can cause the shotgun to become unsafe in any way (simultaneous discharge, faulty trigger, breech lock insecure etc.) shall be declared unsafe by the referee and shall not be used further in the event until properly repaired.

(e) Procedure in the event of a malfunction. The competitor shall without turning from the firing mark, touching the safety catch, opening the gun or interfering with the mechanism of the gun in any way, hand his gun *safely* to the referee for the referee to inspect and give his decision.

Should the shooter fail in any of these respects the target shall be declared lost.

Misfire (*see* Malfunction)

Failure of the cartridge to fire or function properly after the firing pin has made proper contact with the cartridge cap (*see* Penalties and Safety).

The referee shall announce a misfire and declare a no bird:

(a) (i) Where the powder charge fails to ignite.

   (ii) Where the powder charge having ignited fails to propel the shot properly. (This is characterised by a weak report, lack of recoil and *at times* leaves components of the cartridge in the barrel.)

(b) A shooter is allowed a total of two misfires (*or* malfunctions) in any one stage. Thereafter he must abide by the result.

(c) Second barrel misfire. An allowable misfire on the second shot shall be resolved by:

   (i) The target being declared a no bird.

   (ii) the competitor shall then repeat the target and the result of the second shot only shall be scored.

(The shooter must fire the first barrel in the air before firing the second barrel. If the target is killed by the first barrel shot the target will be declared lost.)

(d) Procedure. Any shotgun which has a malfunction which can cause the shotgun to become unsafe in any way (simultaneous discharge, faulty trigger, breech lock insecure etc.) shall be declared unsafe by the referee and shall not be used further in the event until properly repaired.

No bird

After a target has been declared a no bird it is no longer part of the competition and no record of any hits or misses at any no bird is recorded or is of any account.

(a) General. The referee shall declare a no bird and another target shall be allowed only if:

   (i) The competitor shoots out of turn.

   (ii) More than one person shoots at the same target.

   (iii) A shooter shoots from the wrong firing mark.

   (iv) A broken target is thrown.

   (v) An initial foot fault occurs in any stage (*see* Firing Marks and Penalties).

   (vi) More than one target is thrown in single-rise shooting.

(vii) A simultaneous discharge occurs.

(viii) A clay target of an entirely different colour to those used elsewhere in the competition is suddenly thrown.

(ix) In the opinion of the referee, some occurrence takes place that may materially affect the equity of the competition.

Other than the above: *If a shooter fires one or both barrels at a whole target in flight the result shall be scored.*

(b) Target Refused. A no bird shall be declared if the shooter *has not fired (or if the referee calls a no bird before or as the shooter fires his first shot.)* If:

(i) The target appears before or at an interval of time after the shooter's call.

(ii) The target is thrown at a widely different angle.

(c) Claims for a no bird. When a referee does not declare a no bird and the competitor in question considers that he should be awarded a no bird, he must consult with the referee immediately after the shot or target in question. *If this is not done no subsequent calls will be entertained.*

If after this the shooter is still not satisfied with the referee's decision a mark shall be made on the score sheet at the appropriate point for possible later consideration by the jury.

Official score

This is the score, having been properly recorded by a person or persons authorised to do so, finally agreed and posted on the main scoreboard.

Penalties

Where imposed, shall apply for all purposes.

(a) (i) Shall be imposed by the jury only.

(ii) May take the form of a warning, loss of points or disqualification.

(iii) In serious cases the matter shall be referred to the Association for possible disciplinary action.

(b) A warning will be given by the referee for initial minor transgressions in safety and behaviour. The referee shall give a warning which shall be recorded on the score card for a competitor's:

(i) First foot fault in any one stage.

(ii) For the first or second misfire or malfunction in any one stage.

(iii) First interval exceeding 15 seconds before calling in any one stage.

(c) One point deduction. The jury shall deduct one point from a competitor's score for:

(i) The second and each subsequent foot fault in any one stage.

(ii) Each interruption to the sequence of shooting due to insufficient cartridges having been brought to the firing mark.

(iii) The second and each subsequent interval in excess of 15 seconds before calling in any one stage.

(d) Three points deduction. The jury deduct three points from a competitor's score for:

(i) Not being present without sufficient cause at the required place and time after being duly notified.

(ii) Failing to be present to act as scorer or referee in proper turn as required (suitable substitutes may be accepted).

(iii) Any other reason the jury shall deem is in keeping with the spirit of the rules herein.

(e) Disqualification. The jury *may* disqualify a competitor for:

(i) Serious breaches of safety.

(ii) Shooting on the grounds from any place other than the firing marks.

(iii) Shooting at any live bird or beast or at any objects other than the clay targets in flight.

The jury *shall* disqualify a competitor for:

(iv) Being disorderly.

(v) Being intoxicated.

(vi) Any other reason the jury shall deem is in keeping with the spirit of these rules.

Practice shooting

Practice targets shall be of the same make and colour as those used in the competition.

(a) One practice regular target may be shot at by each member of the squad immediately prior to each stage of a registered competition.

(b) Such targets shall be shot at from the firing

marks allotted to each member of the squad in their order shown on the score card.

(c) No practice shooting will take place until the referee has indicated that it is correct and safe to do so.

(d) Practice may be arranged and published by the event organisers for the day or days before the competition.

(e) Practice other than in (a) shall not be permitted on any layout to be used in the event, on the days of competition.

Protests

May be made only by the competitor, his team captain or his team manager.

(a) If the jury so require, shall be submitted in writing together with a fee not exceeding £5 (this shall be returned only if the protest is upheld).

(b) A protest concerning a score or scores must be made immediately after the squad affected has finished shooting.

(c) A protest concerning whether:
  (i) the target was hit or not or by which shot.
  (ii) the shooter was balked
  (iii) the target was an alleged no bird
  (iv) the target was of a widely different colour

must be made immediately after the target or shot in question to the referee in the first instance. If the competitor is still not satisfied with regard to (b), (c) and (d) only he may take his protest to the jury for their consideration.

(d) No protest will be entertained after all the final results have been posted (except for queries regarding the addition of scores).

It would be very much appreciated if all queries and protests could be made in a quiet and orderly manner.

Puller

A person, so authorised, who shall release targets, either electrically or mechanically, immediately after the shooter's call.

(a) He shall have an unobstructed view of the competitors on their firing marks.

(b) He shall have an unobstructed view of the targets in flight.

(c) He shall give his opinion as to whether a target is hit or not when asked *by the referee*.

Referee

A person authorised and competent to adjudicate a stage of a competition in accordance with the rules herein. (*Wherever possible, CPSA referees should be used.*)

(a) The referee's decision on whether a target is killed or not is *final*.

(b) Where there is some doubt as to the result of any shot he shall consult the scorer and puller only and then announce his final decision.

(c) He shall announce the result of shooting at each target distinctly and loudly by calling 'one' for the first barrel kill, 'two' for a second barrel kill, 'lost' when the target remains unbroken or 'no bird' as necessary.

(d) He shall adjudicate the competition fairly and according to the current rules.

(e) He shall ensure and demonstrate if necessary at the start of a stage after a breakdown or complaint that targets are thrown according to the rules herein.

(f) He shall ensure that the competitors shoot according to the rules herein.

(g) He shall have an uninterrupted view of competitors and the clay targets in flight.

(h) He is empowered to challenge the ammunition of any competitor at any time by removing a cartridge for inspection.

(i) He may call upon the jury at any time to arbitrate if he so wishes. He *must* call upon the jury if three or more competitors in the same squad so request, except where the dispute has regard solely to whether a target is killed or lost (*see* (a)).

(j) Where a serious and prolonged mechanical breakdown occurs the referee, in consultation with the jury, shall have the option of standing the squad down to continue at a later time or continuing on another layout. In either case the assembled squad may view, then shoot at one regular target before the competition is resumed.

Refused entry

The management of any shooting ground shall have the right to refuse entry to any person if they are satisfied that such person behaves or is likely to behave in a manner thought to be unsafe or disorderly.

Registered targets

All clay targets shot at from the standard 16 yard mark in certain specified open and approved tournaments are known as 'registered targets'.

(a) Only clubs or grounds affiliated to the Association may hold Registered events.

(b) The Association require the inspection of all layouts before authorising their use for registered events.

(c) The score made at such targets form the basis of the averages for CPSA members for the current classification system.

(d) Where a competitor withdraws or is unable, for any reason, to complete the full programme as specified, the score attained from the number of targets shot at, should be returned as the registered score for such competitor. (The return sheet should be clearly marked to indicate this, eg '66 Kills ex 75 birds 190 pts ex 225 pts'.)

(e) Targets shot at in practice or ties connected with any DTL competition are not regarded as 'registered targets'.

Regular target

A whole clay target thrown in accordance with these rules.

Scoring and scorer

CPSA competitions shall normally be scored using the 'points system' viz: 3 points for a first barrel kill; 2 points for a second barrel kill; 0 points for a target not hit by either shot.

(a) The scorer shall keep an accurate record of the result of shots at each target.

(b) He shall mark the score card '1' for 'kill 1', '2' for 'kill 2' and '0' for a lost target as the referee so calls.

(c) He shall give his opinion as to whether a target is hit or not when asked *by the referee*.

(d) He shall mark the score card appropriately to record misfires, malfunctions, foot faults or safety warnings or interruptions as the referee so directs (viz: MIS, MAL, FF, SW, INT).

(e) He shall total the number of kills and points accurately at the completion of the required number of targets.

(f) He shall announce the final scores aloud to the referee and assembled squad.

(g) He shall sign and ask the referee to countersign the score card when the scores are finalised.

(h) Each member of the squad is entitled to inspect the completed score card before it is taken for posting to the main scoreboard.

Setting the trap

1 **Datum Point**
   (a) All measurements are taken with reference to the top surface of firing mark No. 3 (the datum point).
   (b) Allowances must be made where the ground is at a different level to this datum.
   (c) Distances, where given, are all measured from the centre of the pivot point of the trap where it is set to throw a straight away target.
   (d) Care should be taken that traps are set in still weather; slight adjustments may be necessary in certain wind conditions.

2 **Target Height**. At a distance of 10 yards (9m) from the trap, a regular target shall attain a height of 8 to 10 feet (2.44–3.05m). To ensure the correct elevation, procure an 8 foot pole with a loop 2 foot (61cm) diameter attached to the top end. Place the pole upright at 10 measured yards in front of the trap. The trap should then be set to throw the target through the loop centre.

   A dumpy level, or similar, should be used to ensure that the correct measuring height is attained 10 yards from the trap; eg: with rising ground from the trap it may be found that the ground has risen 2 feet at a point of

10 yards from the trap. It will then be necessary to have this measuring pole 6 feet (1.82m) long and not 8 feet for that layout.

3 **Target Flight**. A regular target shall travel a distance of 45.7m to 50.3m (50 to 55 yards).

4 **Angles**
    (a) (i) The targets shall be thrown randomly within an area bounded by an angle of 22 degrees either side of an imaginary straight line drawn through the centre of firing mark No. 3, and projected past the centre of the pivot point of the trap when it is set to throw a straight away target.
      (ii) *The trap shall be set at this angle to the left and to the right of this straight line for all registered events.*

Note: These angles can be visibly checked by noting that with the trap set to throw an extreme left hand target this would appear as a straight away bird when viewed from firing mark No. 5 and for an extreme right hand target as a straight away bird when viewed from firing mark No. 1.

    (b) To allow for unfavourable wind conditions, an additional tolerance of 10 degrees either side of the 22½ degree angles (in 4(a)(i)) left and right shall be considered as the boundary defining a widely different angle and two posts set at these further angles shall be placed about 30m (35 yards) from the trap. Targets thrown within this area shall be considered to be within bounds.

5 **Recommendation.** The trap should be set so that the tip of the throwing arm, in the released position, is about 50cm (18m) above ground level.

Simultaneous discharge

When, for any cause, both barrels are discharged together or almost together (*see* 'No bird' (a)(viii)).

Stage

One part, division or section of a competition (usually 25 targets per competitor but *see* 'DTL Procedure' 9.

Squad

A number of competitors (usually five) whose names appear together on the same score card, to shoot the same stage on the same layout at the same time. *Squads comprising more than five competitors are prohibited.*

(a) They shall occupy the firing marks in the order their names are listed on the score cards

(b) Competitors shall be arranged in squads of five except:
    (i) When there are fewer than five competitors available.
    (ii) When a competitor withdraws from the competition after it has begun.
    (iii) When there is a shoot-off involving less than five competitors.

(c) The squad, when assembled and before any shooting commences at each stage, is permitted to view a regular target (*see* 'Practice shooting'.)

(d) The squad or a member of the squad may request to view a regular target after three consecutive broken targets have been thrown, or after a technical breakdown, or after a complaint regarding target flight angle or distance has been upheld by the referee or jury.

(e) No member of the squad shall move to his next firing point until the call of 'change'.

(f) Members of the squad shall remain at the firing marks until the last shot of the stage is fired.

Targets

Used in all DTL registered events shall conform to the listed specification and colours.

(a) Specifications. Diameter 109-111mm. Height 25-26mm. Weight 100-110g.

(b) Colours permitted: all black, all white, all yellow, all orange or the ring or dome of the target may be painted white, yellow or orange. The colour of targets used should be that which is most visible against the shooting background.

Ties

1 **General**. All ties shall, wherever possible, be shot off in a manner the management deem best fitted to preserve the equity of the competition. A competitor who is absent for a shoot-off shall lose by defualt.

2 **Shoot-offs**
  (a) To decide ties, shoot-offs must take place to decide winners of championships, sections and classes, where there are titles, trophies or special prizes for such championship classes or sections.
  (b) Shoot-offs shall normally take place over stages of 25 birds.

3 **Add and divide**. Where cash prizes are awarded this system saves the necessity for shooting off. The cash prizes to be awarded in the tie are added together and divided equally between the number of competitors in the tie. For example, assume a tie for second and third places, add the prize money for second and third places together and divide this sum equally between the two competitors concerned.

Trap

A device constructed to properly throw a clay target the prescribed height, angle and distance.

1 **Traps suitable for DTL**
  (a) Any type of automatic angling trap that can properly throw targets to the specifications required for DTL, may be used.
  (b) The trap must be capable of throwing targets at unknown angles, within the specifications for DTL and which cannot be predetermined.
  (c) Recommendation. Great care should be taken in selecting a suitable trap for DTL. Such machines have to cope with a great number of targets in a very short time. Choose a type that is capable of throwing a good target consistently and reliably.

2 **Types Available**
  (a) *Manually operated*. These machines are comparatively cheap to buy and with good servicing will give many years of service. They are usually easily converted for double-rise. Installation: care must be taken to ensure a firm and level base for the cocking lever. Follow the makers' instructions carefully. Operation: these machines require two operations – one to load the machine and one to operate the cocking and release lever.
  (b) *Electrically operated traps*. These usually operate on a continuously angling basis. They are long lasting and trouble free. Installation: the machine only has to be bolted down on to a suitable base which should preferably be concrete, faced with wood. Operation: these machines require two operators – one operator situated in the trap house to load the target and one operator standing behind the shooter with the release button.
  (c) *Electrically operated auto-loading traps*. These machines are reliable, efficient and can give long and trouble-free service. Installation: the machine need only be placed on a level surface and does not require more than nominal fixing, its weight being adequate to keep it in place. Operation: these machines require one operator if used with the push button system. If used with acoustic release they may well operate perfectly without operators. Capacity is about 350 targets, adequate for two complete squads without refilling.

  Certain types of these machines can be used equally well for automatic ball trap, the change-over taking perhaps five minutes.

Limitations. Traps with automatic loading, angling, cocking and firing devices are not suitable for double-rise.

Unfinished competition

(a) Should any competition fail to be completed due to extreme bad weather, darkness or major equipment failure then the competition jury may suspend the event.

(b) Before the jury disbands, it shall announce publicly at the suspended shoot a date at and the terms under which the competition shall continue. Such date should not be more than four weeks from the date of the original competition.

(c) Any competitor who fails to attend on the new date set for the postponed competition shall forfeit all rights and standing in the competition. No refund of entry fee need be paid.

(d) Not withstanding the above, the jury may decide to end the competition and award prizes at some point equitable with fair play. The jury in this case may recommend to the management a proportional refund of entry fees paid.

Widely different angle

A target that travels outside the prescribed extreme limit indicating posts.

Double-rise

In this type of shooting two targets are released simultaneously and the shooter fires one shot at each target. He scores five points for killing both targets, two points for killing one target or zero points for failing to kill either.

The trap angle does not alter as in single-rise shooting but is fixed near centrally to give the required flight and angles.

Regulations. Except where otherwise indicated the general regulations given for single-rise events will normally apply. There are obvious differences in some instances and the following shall apply in respect of some particular regulations not quite so self-evident.

Flight Angles. Set the trap to throw the targets as near as possible on the 22½ degree line one to the left and one to the right at equal angles from the centre line.

No Birds

(a) The referee shall declare *the pair no bird* when:

    (i) One target only is thrown.

    (ii) Two targets are killed with one shot.

    (iii) Either or both targets are thrown broken.

    (iv) One target follows the other at an interval of time.

    (v) An allowable misfire or malfunction occurs on either target.

    (vi) The flight of either is outside the prescribed limits and the competitor has not yet fired a shot.

    (vii) The shooter *refuses* the first target and *does not shoot* at all.

    (viii) The shooter having shot at and killed the first target then refuses the second target.

In all such cases a repeat pair will be thrown to determine the results of *both shots*.

(b) (i) If the shooter having shot at the first target and missed then refuses the second target, the pair shall be repeated to determine the result of the second shot only, the result of the first target being scored lost.

    (ii) In such case, the shooter must be seen by the referee to shoot at the first target before shooting at the second target. If the shooter fails in this, the result shall be scored lost & lost.

(c) *If a shooter shoots at both targets in flight the result shall be scored.* (Unless the referee calls 'no bird' before or as the shooter fires at either target.)

Ties

As for single-rise except that it is usual to shoot at ten or five pairs per competitor.

One-shot-per-target

A competitor shall shoot once only at each target. If a competitor misses the first target with his first shot and hits the same target with the second shot the *referee shall declare both birds lost*.

Safety (*see* Penalties)

It is the responsibility of all shotgun users to behave in a safe manner at all times.

(a) Treat every gun as if it is loaded.

(b) Carried guns must be open and empty at all times except when about to be fired at the proper time and place.

(c) Keep the muzzles of all guns pointed up range at all times when the gun is closed.

(d) In the event of a misfire or malfunction the gun muzzles must be kept pointing toward a safe area.

(e) When 'clearing' guns, never shoot at the ground or near the trap house.

Unsafe gun handling can be fatal!

ENGLISH SKEET

Layout

For illustration of layout see Chapter 11.

Targets

1. One target should emerge from a trap house (called High House) at a point 91cm beyond the Station Marker One (measured along the base chord extended) and 3.05m above the ground level. The other target should emerge from a trap house (called Low House) at a point 91cm beyond Station Marker Seven (measured along the base chord extended), and 76cm from the base chord extended (measured on the side of the target crossing point) and 1m above the ground. The targets shall fly a distance of 50m to 52m.

2. Targets used shall comply with ISU Rules.

3. **A Regular Target.** This is one which appears instantly when the shooter calls, and passes within the specified points.

4. **An Irregular Target**

(a) An unbroken target which has not conformed to the definition of a regular target.

(b) Two targets thrown simultaneously in singles.

(c) Targets thrown broken: under no circumstances shall the result of firing upon a broken target be counted.

5. **Regular Doubles.** A regular target thrown from each trap house simultaneously.

6. **Irregular Doubles**

(a) If either or both targets of a double are thrown as irregular targets

(b) If only one target is thrown.

Organisation of competitions

7. Firing is normally conducted in groups of five competitors each. If it becomes necessary, groups of less than five members may be formed but groups of more than six must be avoided for control and safety reasons.

8. The following targets will be shot:

Station One – two singles and a double
Station Two – two singles and a double
Station Three – two singles
Station Four – two singles and a double (the shooter must nominate the first target of the double)
Station Five – two singles
Station Six – two singles and a double
Station Seven – two singles and a double.
Optional or repeat target – first target missed or a single either high or low from Station Seven. This shall be scored as the twenty-fifth shot.

9. The first target to be shot on Stations One and Two doubles will be the high house, and on stations Six and Seven it shall be the low house.

10. Each shooter shall complete his shooting on one stand before leaving the stand.

11. At the beginning of each round when the squad is assembled at Station One, they shall be entitled to observe one regular target from each trap house. A competitor may also ask to have one regular target thrown after each irregular target, except when the irregular target was fired at.

12. If a shooter is not present when his squad is called, the referee must call the name three times loudly within the period of one minute. If he does

not appear then, the shooting shall start without him (Article 50). In order to be eligible to shoot in that round, a late member must arrive in time to shoot his first bird before the No. 1 man of his squad has taken his position at Station Two.

13. If a breakdown occurs to a trap during the shooting, the referee will decide if the shooting will be continued on another field or on the same field after the breakdown has been repaired. The squad shall be entitled to observe one regular target from each trap house before the shooting continues.

Referees and jury

14. The shooting shall be conducted by a referee with wide experience in skeet shooting. His main function is to make immediate decisions regarding 'dead' or 'lost' targets, and he is to give a distinct signal for all lost targets.

15. The referee shall make an immediate decision whether a repeat target is to be thrown due to an irregular target or some other reason. If possible he shall call 'no bird' before the shooter has fired his first shot.

16. A jury shall be formed consisting of five members representative of the competing shooters, who shall elect a chairman.

The jury shall make decisions by majority vote. The jury can make decisions when the chairman and two jury members are present to vote. As an exception in urgent cases two members who agree upon a decision may act as a valid jury after having consulted with the referee.

17. It is the duty of the jury:
(a) To ascertain that the ranges and the targets thrown conform to regulations.
(b) To see, during the shooting, that the rules are adhered to and to examine the guns, ammunition, and targets by random tests or other suitable procedures.
(c) To make decisions in connection with technical defects or other disturbances in the shooting, if these are not made by the referee.

(d) To deal with protests.
(e) To make decisions regarding penalty if a shooter does not adhere to the regulations or conducts himself in an unsportsmanlike manner.
(f) To agree on a plan so that at least two jury members are always present on the range.

Guns and ammunition

18. All types of guns, including automatics, 12 gauge and smaller may be used for shooting. No handicap will be given to competitors using guns of a calibre smaller than 12 gauge (Art. 49).

Changing of guns (or properly functioning parts) between stations within a round is not permitted unless the referee has accepted a gun malfunction which cannot be quickly repaired.

19. The length of the cartridge, before being fired, not to exceed 70mm (except for ·410 cartridges). The shot load not to exceed 32 gm or size to exceed size of No. 9 shot (English). Cartridges must be of normal loading, no internal changes may be made. Each round of skeet will be completed with cartridges of one type only, those being the ones with which the round was started, different loads or shot sizes will not be used within the round. (The referee may at any time remove an unfired cartridge from a shooter's gun for inspection.) Black powder and tracer cartridges are forbidden.

20. When a gun fails to function and the referee on inspection finds that it is disabled in such manner as to render it not quickly repairable, and that this has not been caused by the shooter himself, the shooter should have the option of using another gun if one can be secured without delay, or dropping out of the squad and finishing the remaining shots at a later time when a vacancy occurs and the refereee gives his permission. If his gun is repaired before the end of the round, the shooter may be permitted to rejoin the squad providing the referee gives his permission. In other cases of malfunction of either guns or ammunition which result in the shot not leaving the gun (provided this is not the fault of the shooter) he has the choice of changing his gun or

continuing with the same one. A competitor is allowed two repeat targets (malfunctions of gun and ammunition combined) during each round of 25 targets, one for each malfunction whether he has changed his gun or not.

A shot will be considered a misfire (valid malfunction) if there is no detonation after the primer has been struck. Should the shooter not release the trigger sufficiently to fire the second cartridge of a double or to cause (automatic) fan-firing, this will be considered a fault of the shooter and will not entitle him to a repeat target.

Shooting rules

21. One shot only may be fired at each target during its flight within the shooting bounds – an area 40.2m in front of the traphouse from which the target is thrown.

22. Shooting position: standing with both feet entirely within the boundary of the shooting station. Gun position optional.

23. When the shooter is ready to shoot he calls loudly 'pull', 'go', 'ready' or some other signal of command after which the target shall be thrown instantly.

Dead and lost targets

24. A target is declared 'dead' when it is completely destroyed or a visible piece falls as a result of being fired upon according to these regulations. The referee shall be the sole judge of a dead or lost target.

25. The target shall be declared 'lost' if:
(a) The target is not broken or it is hit outside the shooting boundary.
(b) The target is only dusted.
(c) When the target flutters, has insufficient velocity or takes an irregular course on leaving the trap.
(d) When the shooter's position is not according or ammunition occurs to a shooter in a 25 bird round.
(e) When firing a double a competitor is unable

to fire his second shot because he has failed to load a second cartridge; or he has incorrectly set an automatic gun; or the recoil from the first shot has applied the safety catch; or the second round is discharged by the recoil from the first shot; or for any other reason whatsoever.
(f) During doubles, the second shot does not leave because the competitor using single trigger, has not released it sufficiently after the first shot.
(g) After a misfire or malfunction, a competitor touches the safety catch or opens the gun before the referee has inspected it.
(h) The shot is not fired due to some other reason which does not entitle the shooter to a repeat target.
(i) The doubles are fired in inverse order, both targets shall be scored 'lost'.

No bird

26. Under the following circumstances 'no bird' shall be declared and another target thrown whether or not the competitor has fired:
(a) If the target breaks on throwing.
(b) If the target is thrown from the wrong trap house.
(c) If two targets are thrown simultaneously in singles.
(d) If the target is of a colour manifestly different from that of the others used in the competition.
(e) If the first target in doubles is regular and the second is irregular.

27. 'No bird' to be declared and another target thrown if the competitor has not fired:
(a) When the target is thrown before the shooter has called.
(b) When the target does not appear immediately.
(c) When the target flutters, has insufficient velocity or takes an irregular course on leaving the trap.
(d) When the shooter's position is not according to Article 22 and the shooter has not been warned in the round.

No claim of irregularity shall be allowed where targets were actually fired upon and the alleged irregularity consists of deviation from the prescribed line of flight, or because of an alleged 'quick' or 'slow' pull, unless the referee has distinctly called 'no bird' prior to the firing of the shot in the event of the 'quick pull' or prior to the emergence of the target in the event of the 'slow pull'. Otherwise if the shooter fires, the result shall be scored.

28. In the case of misfire or other malfunction of gun or ammunition through no fault of the shooter, 'no bird' shall be declared and a repeat target thrown a maximum of two times for each shooter in a round of 25 targets regardless of whether the shooter changes his gun or not. Upon the third and succeeding malfunctions the targets are scored as lost targets.

29. The referee may also permit a new target to be thrown if:
(a) The shooter has been visibly distracted.
(b) Another shooter fires at the same target.
(c) The referee cannot for some reason decide whether the target was hit or missed.

The referee will not declare a 'no bird' if the shooter misses a target for reasons other than those covered by the rules regarding 'no bird'.

30. The foregoing Articles also apply to doubles and will be interpreted as follows.
(a) The double will be declared 'no bird' and the competitor must shoot a regular double to determine the results of both shots if:
  (i) The first target is regular and the second is irregular regardless of whether the first target is dead or lost.
  (ii) A malfunctioning gun or ammunition prevents the shooter from firing at the first target.
  (iii) Either target of the double is irregular and the shooter does not fire. If the alleged trajectory consists of a deviation from normal, insufficient initial velocity or a fast or slow pull and if both targets have been shot at, the results must be counted.
  (iv) The shooter misses his first target and it collides with the second target before the shooter fires his second shot, or if fragments from the first target break the second target before he has fired his second shot.

(v) The referee prevents the shooter from shooting his second shot because of violation of Article 22. If the shooter has already been warned of the same violation during the same round, the result of the first shot will be recorded and the second target will be declared 'lost'.
(b) Lost targets:
  (i) Upon the third and subsequent malfunction of the gun or faulty ammunition in the same round.
  (ii) If the shooter (without legitimate reason) does not fire at a regular double both targets will be declared 'lost'.
  (iii) If the shooter (without legitimate reason) does not fire at the second target of a regular double, the result of the first target will be recorded and the second target declared 'lost'.
  (iv) If, in a regular double, the first target is lost and the second shot cannot be fired because of a malfunction of the gun or ammunition the first target is scored 'lost' and the double repeated to determine the second result.

31. (a) If, in the course of shooting at doubles, both shots are discharged simultaneously, the double is declared 'no bird' and is repeated as a regular double to determine the results of both shots if the first target was hit.
(b) If the shooter breaks both targets with the same shot, the double will be declared 'no bird' and repeated. The shooter is allowed three attempts on one station. On the fourth attempt if the same situation occurs, the double will be scored 'dead and lost'.
(c) If in shooting at a regular double, the shooter misses the first target and accidentally hits the second target with the same shot, he will be scored 'lost' first target and shoot again at a regular pair of doubles to determine the result of the second shot. The shooter is allowed three attempts on one station. On the fourth attempt if the same situation occurs, the double will be scored 'lost' and 'lost'.

32. Shots will not be scored:
(a) If the shooter fires out of turn.
(b) If the shot is discharged involuntarily before

the shooter has called for his target. Accidental discharges may be cause for penalty or elimination from a competition for unsafe gun handling.

Rules of conduct

33. All guns, even when empty, shall be handled with the greatest of care. Conventional double barrel guns are to be carried with the breech open and the muzzle in a safe direction, up, or down at the ground. Straps or slings on guns are prohibited. When a shooter puts his gun aside it must be placed vertically in a gun stand or another place intended for this purpose. It is forbidden to touch or handle another competitor's gun without the owner's specific permission.

34. Shooting and sighting may only be practised on the shooting station. Shots may only be fired when it is the shooter's turn and the target has been thrown. It is forbidden to sight or shoot at another competitor's targets. It is also forbidden to wilfully sight or shoot at live birds or animals.

35. At roll call before the beginning of a round the shooter must be ready to shoot immediately and take with him sufficient ammunition and other necessary equipment.

36. No member of a squad shall advance to the shooting station until it is his turn to shoot and the previous shooter has left the shooting station. No member of the squad having shot from one station shall proceed towards the next station in such a way as to interfere with another shooter.

37. It is prohibited to place cartridges into any part of the gun before the shooter is standing on the station with the gun pointed in the direction of the target flight area and the referee has indicated that shooting may begin. During shooting of singles it is permitted to load only one cartridge in the gun at a time.

38. If the target is not thrown instantly the shooter is to denote that he refuses the target by remaining 'ready'. (The referee shall be the sole judge of determining a slow or fast pull.)

39. After a shot has been fired or after a regular target has been thrown without the shot being fired the competitor must not turn away from the target flight area before opening his gun. When an irregular target (no bird) is thrown or the shooting interrupted, the gun shall be opened. It is not to be closed again until shooting can continue.

40. In the case of a misfire or other malfunction of gun or ammunition the shooter shall remain standing with the gun pointed to the flight area without opening the gun or touching the safety catch until the referee has inspected the gun.

41. The shooting shall be carried out without interruption. The shooter shall indicate he is ready and call for his targets, or indicate a protest if necessary. The shooter shall answer any of the referee's questions.

42. The referee, under the supervision of the jury shall see that these regulations and safety precautions are adhered to.

Protests

43. A referee shall not be interfered with or interrupted unnecessarily. Verbal or written protests submitted to a member of the jury shall be accompanied by a fee set by the jury. If the protest is upheld then the fee shall be returned.

44. If a competitor disagrees with the referee's decision regarding a shot, protest should be initiated immediately by raising the arm and saying 'protest' or 'appeal'. The referee shall then interrupt the shooting and make his decision. It is not allowed to pick up a target from the field in order to find out whether it has been hit or not.

45. The referee's decision can be appealed against verbally or in writing to the jury. If the jury finds the protest justified it can give the referee directions for future decisions or appoint a new referee, or alter his decision, if this does not concern hits, misses, or irregular targets where the referee's decision is final.

46. If the shooter is of the opinion that the score which is read aloud when the round is finished is incorrect, he should make protest verbally to the referee immediately. The referee shall then, as soon as possible, examine the score sheet, after which he shall announce his decision. If the shooter is not satisfied with the decision, a short written protest shall be made to the jury.

47. If a competitor, or official, observes anything which does not conform to these rules, he must not interfere with the shooting, but shall report his finding to the referee or a member of the jury. Action shall then be taken.

Penalties

48. Every competitor is obligated to acquaint himelf with the rules insofar as they apply to the shooters. By entering the competition he thereby agrees to submit to any penalty that may be incurred through failure to comply with the rules or with the referee's decisions.

49. If the shooter uses guns or ammunition which are not in accordance with Articles 18 and 19, all shots fired with such gun or such ammunition shall be counted as misses. If the jury finds that the fault has been committed with intent, it can in consequence hereof exclude the shooter from the competition. If the jury finds that the shooter could not be reasonably aware of the fault and that he, through the fault, has attained no essential advantage, it can decide to approve the score, providing the fault is corrected as soon as the shooter has become aware of it.

50. If the shooter is not present after the referee has called his name and number three times and this is not due to circumstances beyond his control the shooter is to be fined three birds and given the opportunity to shoot the remaining targets of the round at a time decided by the referee. If the competitor leaves his group for one of the reasons cited in Articles a penalty of one target shall be imposed for each interruption and he shall be permitted to shoot the remaining targets at a later time.

51. Should the jury find that a shooter delays the shooting or conducts himself in an unsportsmanlike manner, it may give him a warning or fine him one bird, or exclude him from the match.

52. When the jury fines a shooter one bird and the decision is not occasioned by any special target, the first dead target after the decision has been made known is to be counted as lost. If the shooter has completed the day's shooting or the whole competition one bird shall be deducted from the score of the last round.

If a shooter has been designated as an assistant referee and is late or fails to present himself or provide an acceptable substitute without delaying the squad, he shall first receive a warning in the case of being late and shall be penalised by one target by the jury if he fails to appear or provide an acceptable substitute.

Ties

53. If two or more shooters obtain equal scores, precedence for the first three places in championships (and in other competitions where this has been announced in the programme) are decided by tie-shooting in 25 bird rounds until a difference in scores occurs. The round or rounds shall be shot according to these rules in such a way, however, that the squads may consist of less than five men. Unless the tie-shooting is to be held at a pre-arranged time, the shooters involved shall keep in touch with the management, so that the tie-shooting can be carried out at the latest 30 minutes after the shooting proper is finished.

54. For the remaining scores the last 25 bird round is to decide precedence; thereafter, the second to last and so forth. If all stages are equal, precedence is decided by counting the last target forward until a zero is found and the shooter with the most hits in succession takes precedence.

55. If two or more teams obtain the same scores ranking will be determined by the total score of the team members in the last series of 25 targets and then next to the last series, until the tie is broken.

Index